D0970566

Five States for Goldwater

BERNARD COSMAN

FIVE STATES
for
GOLDWATER

CONTINUITY AND CHANGE IN SOUTHERN
PRESIDENTIAL VOTING PATTERNS

With an Introductory Essay by Robert B. Highsaw

UNIVERSITY OF ALABAMA PRESS
University, Alabama

150667

Copyright © 1966 by University of Alabama Press:
Library of Congress Catalog Card Number: 66–17568
Manufactured in the United States of America
by Kingsport Press, Inc., Kingsport, Tenn.

Contents

Acknowledgements

Professors Cosman and Highsaw wish to thank the following publishers for granting permission to quote from the publications cited: Alfred A. Knopf, Inc., *Public Opinion and American Democracy* and *Southern Politics* by V. O. Key, Jr., and *The Political System* by David Easton; University of Illinois Press, *Essays on the Behavioral Study of Politics* edited by Austin Ranney;

American Political Science Association, "The Behavioral Approach in Political Science" by Robert A. Dahl, "The Changing Shape of the American Political Universe" by Walter Dean Burnham, and "Electoral Myth and Reality: The 1964 Election" by Philip E. Converse, Aage Clausen, and Warren Miller, all in *The American Political Science Review;* Random House, Inc., *The Behavioral Persuasion in Politics* by Heinz Eulau; Houghton Mifflin Company, *Politics and Social Life* by Nelson W. Polsby, Robert A. Dentler and Paul A. Smith; Duke University Press, *Change in the Contemporary South* edited by Allen P. Sindler; Prentice–Hall, Inc., *The Deadlock of Democracy* by James MacGregor Burns; Thomas Y. Crowell Company, *Politics, Parties and Pressure Groups* by V. O. Key, Jr.; and Southern Regional Council, "What Happened in the South?".

Preface

IN THIS VOLUME I HAVE SOUGHT TO identify certain elements of continuity and change in the presidential voting patterns of southern electorates. One dimension only is treated—that of presidential Republicanism, and this with particular emphasis on the Goldwater outcome in 1964 and its relationship to earlier voting alignments in the South.

Methodologically, I have relied on aggregate data, ordered and analyzed by means of relatively simple arithmetical and statistical procedures. It must be admitted that aggregate data are not of unlimited utility in election research, but perhaps the results of our analysis may serve as yet another reminder that such data do have their valid uses. The methodological strengths and weaknesses of aggregate data in the study of macro– and micro–political behavior are discussed in Professor Robert B. Highsaw's essay on "Interdisciplinary Behavioralism in Election Research" and in my introductory chapter on "The Problem of Continuity and Change in Southern Voting Patterns".

I am especially grateful to Professor Highsaw for his contributions to this volume, and to Professor Donald S. Strong for many helpful comments and suggestions. Appreciation is also due the Bureau of Public Administration, University of Alabama, and to the Eagleton Institute and the National Center for Education in Politics for a National Convention Fellowship that has helped to make the present work possible. I must also acknowledge the invaluable assistance of Mr. George C. Croker, Jr., Mr. George G. Kundahl, and Mr. Irvin Penfield, graduate students in the Department of Political Science, University of Alabama, each of whom assisted at various stages in the collection and ordering of data. As must be, however, the ultimate responsibility for the outcome is mine alone.

BERNARD COSMAN

January 10, 1966
University, Alabama

Interdisciplinary Behavioralism
in Election Research

An Introductory Essay by Robert B. Highsaw

Interdisciplinary Behavioralism in Election Research

An Introductory Essay by Robert B. Highsaw

Eᴌᴇᴄᴛɪᴏɴs ᴀʀᴇ, ᴀs ᴛʜᴇ ʟᴀᴛᴇ V. O. Kᴇʏ pointed out, a "basic means by which the people of a democracy bend government to their wishes".[1] It is through the electoral process that people act collectively by balloting to select their governors and to hold them accountable. The act of voting constitutes the primary means by which most Americans can actively express their political preferences. Indeed, for many Americans voting is the only form of political action.

Since they have an intrinsic importance to democratic systems of governance, elections have been a central concern of those who have sought to develop and enhance understanding of American democracy and politics. Whether viewed as collective decisions or from the standpoint of the individual's vote, elections and the voting behavior which they represent have captured the continuing interest and attention, first, of historians and, more recently, of political scientists, political sociologists, and social psychologists.

For more than a century, electoral studies were primarily descriptive, having as their relevant points of focus candidates, issues, and campaigns, usually at the level of the presidential contest. The tradition of historical–description is an old and very honorable one in the study of political processes, and many of its products have been immensely valuable when measured by their own criteria.[2] However, historical–descriptive studies have directed little systematic attention toward electoral behavior responsive to candidates, issues, and other political stimuli, although official records of national and state elections have been maintained in the case of presidential elections since 1835, and for some state and local elections since the founding of the American federal system.

The lag between the availability of aggregate data and its systematic analysis is explained, in some measure, by the fact that techniques appropriate for its analysis were not developed until the second and third decades of this century. Then, too, there was the fact that it was not until the 1920's and 1930's that the U.S. Bureau of the Census published enough in the way of social characteristics of small areas that voting behavior could be related to these characteristics.[3]

The marriage of statistical method and aggregate data reaped early benefits with the studies of Cortez A. M. Ewing, Harold F. Gosnell, Edward H. Litchfield, James K. Pollock, and Stuart A. Rice, and later with the work of V. O. Key, Alexander Heard, and Donald S. Strong. Suffice it to say for the moment that aggregative analyses have provided a rich, insightful, and, I think it important to add, voluminous body of knowledge about elections and electoral behavior which now extends over four decades. But aggregative studies have suffered from a major deficiency, which is their inability to provide direct access to the individual voter and to the social and psychological processes by which he reaches his electoral decision. It was this deficiency that was remedied by

the development and refinement of the survey
method.

Since its beginnings in the mid–1930's, survey
methodology has provided direct access to the
individual and in a series of landmark studies ini-
tiated with *The People's Choice* and continuing
with *Voting, The Voter Decides,* and *The American Voter,*[4] the application of the survey tech-
nique to the study of presidential elections in the
United States has vastly improved our understanding of electoral behavior and, more recently, has
enhanced our knowledge of the electoral context
within which the individual voter arrives at his
decision to vote and for whom.

In methodology and conceptualization political scientists have much in common with other
social scientists, especially sociologists and social
psychologists. The study of elections and electoral
behavior, in particular, has been an interdisciplinary endeavor, with political scientists freely
drawing upon other disciplines for methods and
concepts that have seemed relevant to the study of
voting behavior. Within the framework of the
discipline of political science, the study of voting
behavior is the oldest and most productive example of the application of what is almost uni-
versally referred to as the behavioral approach.

The behavioral approach in political science
has as its antecedents developments in the natural

sciences and other social sciences, and the dissatisfaction of students of political science with the mood and methods of their discipline in relation to what was being done in other fields. Evron M. Kirkpatrick describes the emergence of dissatisfaction with the state of the discipline in this way:

Influenced by developments in the natural sciences, and perhaps even more by students of the scientific method like Morris Cohen, methodologists within and without the profession found reason for dissatisfaction with what was being done and with the order of findings that resulted. They called attention to the lack of recognition on the part of political scientists of the developments in the other sciences of man, particularly psychology, sociology, anthropology, and psychiatry; they were unhappy about the bulging inventory of facts that had no relation to a comprehensive theory; they noted the extent to which untenable assumptions and premises influenced and distorted findings; they criticized the failure to make better use of statistics and the statistical method; they called attention to the amount of so-called political science that served no function except to bolster the value preferences of the author; they made explicit the low level of generalization of findings; they pointed to the incomparability of much of the data collected; they made clear the difficulty of using the data of political science as it existed for accurate prediction. In brief, many of them accused the profession of dignifying sloppy, impressionistic, crudely empirical, and prejudiced research and writing with the name of science. Dissatisfaction produced ferment, and ferment, change. The challenge to traditional political science resulting from this dissatisfaction probably deserves to be ranked as the most important single recent development in political science.[5]

While political scientists have yet to agree on a precise definition of what is meant by political behavior, there does now appear to have developed a consensus of what are the principal components of the behavioral approach.

In the first instance, the behavioral approach is said to focus on the individual. As David Easton, explaining the meaning of political behavioralism, puts it: "It is clear that this term indicates that the research worker wishes to look at participants in the political system as individuals . . ." [6] Similarly, David B. Truman insists that "political behavior is not and should not be a speciality, for it represents rather an orientation or a point of view which aims at stating all the phenomena of government in terms of the observed and observable behavior of men".[7] Heinz Eulau puts the matter with rare succinctness when he says: "The root is man." [8]

In view of this emphasis upon the individual as the primary unit of analysis, it is not surprising that the behavioral approach also has an interdisciplinary outlook, in which the unity of the social and behavioral sciences is stressed. Thus, the interdisciplinary component of the behavioral approach follows quite naturally from the "very simple assumption that man's political behavior is only one aspect of his total behavior . . ." [9] It follows that behavioralists regard the methods and concepts of the social sciences as common property to be used by any or all, as may be appropriate to the objects of their inquiries.

Attention to method is a third dimension of the behavioral approach. Behavioralism emphasizes quantification and the development and continuous refinement, improvement and elaboration of methodology for use in collecting, ordering, and interpreting political data. "The student of political behavior", writes Truman, ". . . is obliged to perform his task in quantitative terms if he can and in qualitative terms if he must." [10] But the emphasis on methodology is not undertaken for its own sake; rather, attention to methodology permits a more precise specification of hypotheses which, when verified by rigorous methods, may give rise to generalizations predictive of man's behavior, through time and at single points in time.

The behavioralist is, in short, theory–oriented. "Crude empiricism," Truman maintains, "is almost certain to be sterile. Equally fruitless is speculation which is not or cannot be put to empirical test." [11] With systematic political theory based on empirical analysis as their goal, it is not surprising that political behavioralists generally renounce any attempt to prescribe how men *ought* to behave and instead give emphasis to how men *do* behave. More often than not behavioralists will refer to behavior in the "real world", a term which Nelson W. Polsby, for example, defines as consisting of "things and events which more than one competent observer can 'see' and report on".[12]

The *is*–orientation of political behavioralism is manifested in the concern of the political behavioralists with values and the value–problem. The political behavioralist is especially conscious of the place of personal values in the field of political science and their importance to research in political science. The preoccupation of the behavioralists with values and value judgments in the discipline has directed attention to the need of the investigator to specify both his own values and values implicit in his methodology. Their concern with value–problems has led behavioralists to stigmatize traditional descriptive, institutional, and functional methodologies as "value–laden". These criticisms have, in turn, brought forth objections that political behavioralists are lacking in values.

Other objections to political behavioralism have included, in addition to questions of the value of this approach, questions about the application of "scientific" techniques to human behavior which, say the critics, is too complex and unpredictable to permit "scientific study"; questions relating to the jargon of the behavioralists; and questions relating to the objects of behavioral inquiry. Among all of these and other objections to behavioralism, perhaps the most telling criticism is the first—that political behavioralism has not made a contribution to the total body of knowledge of the discipline that is at all commensurate with its promises.[13]

Robert A. Dahl probably is correct when he writes that it is "a little early to appraise the results. We shall need another generation of work before we can put the products of this new mood and outlook in political science in perspective." [14] But if a final appraisal of the merits of behavioralism is not yet feasible, tentative assessments of its possible contribution to the discipline are entirely in order—as has been shown in the work of Dahl, Kirkpatrick, Truman, and others.

Although behavioral studies have been appearing in all fields of political science at a rapidly accelerating rate, most commentators on the

contribution of behavioralism to political science
agree that it is in the area of research into elections and voting that interdisciplinary behavioralism has made the most impressive contribution to
the discipline. But the sheer volume of election and
voting research makes its classification difficult.[15]

In the most general sense we can differentiate
voting studies in terms of the data with which they
are concerned, the methodologies which they employ, and the range and breadth of the hypotheses
with which they are concerned. Thus, if data and
method are the criteria, voting studies may be
said to divide, though not always easily, into two
broad categories: those based on aggregate data
and those that rely on survey data. In a basic way,
studies that fit into these two categories are also
differentiated by method, with the former relying
upon arithmetical and statistical methods, while
the latter, also relying upon these methods, have as
their core survey methodology.

At one time, we could also differentiate among
voting studies along the lines of macro–political
analysis (mass behavior) and micro–political
analysis (individual behavior). The former were
usually based on arithmetical and statistical
analysis, the latter on the results of survey data
and method. However, since survey research has
now focused on macro– as well as micro–political
behavior, such a distinction is no longer a viable

one. At this stage in the development of election and voting research, it is probably appropriate to differentiate voting studies along the lines of data, method, and areal coverage, as well as in terms of the range and breadth of hypotheses stated and tested.

Thus, in studies based on aggregative data, arithmetical and statistical methods are used in analyzing the vote, or "outcome", in particular electoral subdivisions (usually smaller than the nation), using hypotheses of a lower level of generality and sophistication than those used in studies that are based on survey method. But, despite their limitations, aggregative studies have made and continue to make important contributions to the total body of knowledge about elections and voting behavior, particularly at the level of the state and its subdivisions—areas that are difficult to study by means of national surveys. Moreover, aggregative studies have the obvious advantage of availability over a period of time. Indeed, aggregate returns provide the *only* source of data about mass electoral behavior previous to the 1930's.

Professor Bernard Cosman's inquiry into continuity and change in southern Republican presidential voting patterns is an aggregative study that has as its specific focus the 1964 presidential election in the South, particularly with respect to the relationship of voting patterns emerging from that election to those of previous presidential elections in the region. The study fits broadly the genre of research into southern politics, of which V. O. Key's *Southern Politics* and Alexander Heard's *A Two–Party South?* stand as landmarks for the period ending with the decade of the 1940's, while Donald S. Strong's *The 1952 Presidential Election in the South* and *Urban Republicanism* [16] treat the emergent Republicanism of the 1950's. The Key and Heard researches merit description as seminal works for the pre–Eisenhower period, for they embrace the total party organization of the region. Indeed not atypical is the description of Key's research as the "single most influential and valuable work on the American parties" of the last thirty years.[17] Heard, on the other hand, developed the place of the Republican Party in the South, examining its historical position, assessing the prospects for its growth, and, perhaps most importantly, identifying the obstacles that stood in the way of its advance to a position of a viable second party, capable not only of advancing candidates but also of winning elections with some regularity.

Heard's research into Republicanism in the South stopped at a point in time just prior to General Dwight D. Eisenhower's election to the presidency as a Republican. Thus, Heard was deprived of the opportunity to consider the impact of Eisenhower's candidacy upon southern electorates. It was a colleague, Donald S. Strong, who was the first to tap analytically the nature of the developing presidential Republicanism of the 1950's and to determine that the response to Eisenhower rested not only on his personal appeal, but also reflected the translation of socio–economic changes into changing patterns of political balloting, especially in the larger cities. Strong's studies, first of the 1952 presidential election and then of the 1956 election, revealed that Eisenhower, while he attracted remarkably high levels of support throughout the region, was attracting his heaviest support from the cities and, within the cities, from the more prosperous white urbanites. "They're acting like Yankees", is the way Strong described the voting behavior of upper–income white voters.[18]

The researches into southern electoral behavior of Key, Heard, and Strong were based upon aggregative data. The techniques employed by Key and Heard were primarily arithmetical, involving such devices as paired maps, quartile analysis, scatter diagrams, and construction of time–series. Strong, in his study of the 1952 election, relied upon quartile analysis for his survey of statewide voting patterns. For 1956, however, Strong developed a two–way division of the southern states into urban and non–urban sectors, and compared Republican strength within each sector at a single point in time (1956) and over a period of time (1936 to 1956). Strong also studied socio–economic data in relation to the presidential vote within political sub–divisions of selected southern cities, in order to locate and to group patterns of the vote (if any) reflecting socio–economic factors.

Professor Bernard Cosman has built upon the Strong analyses in his study of "Presidential Republicanism in the South, 1960".[19] Now, in his study of the South in the 1964 presidential election, *Five States for Goldwater,* he has used as his structural framework a division of the South, its subregions, and its states, into four sectors: traditionally–Republican, metropolitan, non–metropolitan, and black–belt. Having given this structure to the election returns, Cosman has examined systematically the relationship of the Goldwater vote to pre–1964 voter alignments at the regional, subregional, and state–wide levels. Though the temporal perspective of the study reaches back to 1920, he has given most of his attention to comparison of the voting patterns of 1964 and those of the Eisenhower–Nixon period. In addition to examining the Republican vote over four decades, the author has also focused his attention on the interrelationship of the Goldwater vote and recent third party movements in the South, and especially in the Deep South.

The author's methods for analyzing election returns were primarily arithmetical, though considerable reliance was also placed on simple correlation techniques in order to ascertain the interrelationship of Republican voting at the statewide level over a period of years, and to relate the presidential Republicanism of 1964 with third party support also at the statewide level. He used block data from the 1960 U.S. census of housing to characterize wards and precincts by economic level and racial composition so that he could relate these demographic characteristics to the vote. This interest in socio–economic variables—religion, race, economic status—and his use of these variables to develop classifications of counties, wards, and precincts, is true to the traditional mold of voting–behavior studies based on aggregate data. In this regard, Cosman's analysis is somewhat less sophisticated than studies based on aggregate data in which use has been made of the techniques of multivariate analysis and factoring, both of which have been shown to have the potential of enlarging considerably our understanding of electoral behavior through aggregate data.

In addition to the promise of greater yield in both the quantity and quality of findings that we may reasonably anticipate from a rapidly developing methodology and its dissemination within disciplines, there is also underway the construction of a national electoral–data archive. When completed, this archive should provide the raw materials for what Walter Dean Burnham calls "a massive breakthrough in the behavioral analysis of American political history over the last century and a half".[20] The compilation of a data archive should make it possible to employ both the aggregate and survey approaches so as to make the best possible use of their respective analytical strengths. However, the archive is as yet merely a future expectation. The present reality of electoral research is that we need studies of political behavior in the South—studies of not only the behavior of the southern electorates, but of the region's total political system, as well.

The research reported in *Five States for Goldwater* was concerned with only one component of the political system, the voters. The book deals with the southern electorate's response to Goldwater in terms of both the cyclical characteristics of that response and its secular components, and it raises questions about the nature and possible consequences of changes in patterns of micro–political behavior within the region. These questions, Cosman suggests, can be answered only with electoral data from 1966 and after—and preferably with survey data. Apart from the recent researches of Donald R. Matthews and James W. Prothro,[21] surveys have not always permitted valid generalizations about voting behavior within the region, and certainly not at the state or local level. Because of a lack of data on the subject of micro–political behavior in the South, there remain to be answered a vast number of questions about the nature and shape of politics and political change, particularly in the Deep South.

It is scarcely news to report that the South is undergoing significant economic and social changes, and there are well-validated indications that many of them have already been translated into changes in political balloting. Other political changes, apart from voting divisions, also are taking place—in the composition, size, and quality of electorates; in the recruitment and training of candidates; in the opportunities available to political parties and in the constraints which the system imposes upon them; in the composition of representative bodies.

These changes, of course, are but a few of the alterations now taking place in the components of the region's politics. In many ways, the South is sharing in a transition occurring throughout much of the nation, i.e., a shift in the base of representation from rural to urban areas. In some ways, however, the changes which are taking place in the South—for example, the growth of the

Republican Party and the introduction of
Negroes into regional and subregional electorates
—are almost assuredly of a distinctively southern
character, and may be expected to evoke a
peculiarly southern response. "Members of human societies", writes Philip E. Converse, "are
rather adept at muffling and hedging in such
change as cannot be avoided. Man seems to re-
spond as slowly and narrowly as the situation
permits, and what the situation permits is often
surprising." [22]

For social scientists, the South in the latter half
of the mid–twentieth century presents a labora-
tory for the study of change. For the political
scientist, the opportunities are especially rich and
diverse. Professor Cosman has examined change
and continuity in the region's presidential politics,
but countless opportunties exist for further research. They are found in the area of electoral
behavior, and, perhaps still more fruitfully, in the
areas of legislative, judicial, and adminis-
trative behavior; and they are evident in political
recruitment and training as well as in community
power structure analysis—to mention but a few of
the possibilities.

The methodologies for attacking the problems
can be as rich and diverse as the problems
themselves. Necessarily, the starting point is
broad—"man and his behavior"—but there is

plenty of room for not only the behavioralist and his surveys, arithmetical and statistical analyses, scales, content analyses, models, conceptualizations, and other measurement and analytical techniques, but also for "traditional" political scientists whose methodological orientation is descriptive and functional. Indeed, the latter working together with the former in common endeavor constitutes the best hope for a rich yield of hypotheses whose testing and ultimate verification may bring about truly significant advances in our understanding of political behavior.

ROBERT B. HIGHSAW

January 1, 1966
University, Alabama

Five States for Goldwater

The Problem
of Continuity and Change
in Southern Voting Patterns

NINETEEN SIXTY–FOUR WAS THE YEAR of the South in the Republican presidential party. In the country as a whole, President Lyndon B. Johnson won by a landslide. The Republican candidate, Senator Barry M. Goldwater of Arizona, emerged as a winner in only six states, of which five were in the South. These states were of the region that for almost a century had pro-

vided the Democratic party with its most reliable
bloc of electoral votes. The South may not always
have been safe for the Democrats, but only twice
since the Civil War had the Republicans carried as
many states of this region.

The chronic weakness of southern Republicanism has long been a familiar feature of the American political landscape, one that has been justified
repeatedly by studies of interparty competition
within the states.[1] Regardless of the criteria used
in their investigations, political analysts have invariably found the eleven southern states to be
among the least competitive ones from the Republican standpoint. Put in the usual way, most
southerners voted for Democrats most of the time.

Yet even casual observers have long known that
at the level of presidential politics the South has
not been unswervingly loyal to the Democrats. As
early as 1928, the majority of voters in five southern states broke with tradition to support the
Republican candidate, Herbert Hoover. There
then ensued a period of twenty–four years of Democratic solidarity, broken only in 1948, when the
majority of voters in four southern states rallied
to the standard of the States' Rights Party carried
by J. Strom Thurmond. But the limited success
of this protest party did not represent a break
with southern political tradition; it was, in fact, a
vehement re-affirmation of the past. Four years

later southern voters defected in great numbers from the traditional party of the South in favor of a Republican candidate, enabling Dwight D. Eisenhower to win four states. In 1956, he carried five. Richard M. Nixon won only three states in 1960, but even this more modest success invited continued speculation that the solid South was no more.

It was against this background of an eroding southern commitment to the Democratic presidential party that Senator Goldwater captured five states of the late Confederacy. Given the earlier breakthroughs of Eisenhower and Nixon, it was hardly surprising that Goldwater should make inroads into what had been a Democratic heartland. The novelty of the 1964 presidential outcome lay in the fact that five out of six states won by the Republican presidential party candidate were southern states. At its previous low point of 1936, the Grand Old Party's presidential aspirant, Alf Landon, had received the electoral votes of only two states, but they were Maine and Vermont. Goldwater won more electoral votes than Landon, but never before had a Republican presidential candidate garnered almost all of his electoral votes in the South while at the same time losing in so reliably a Republican state as Vermont.

That 1964 might well be the year of the Republicans in the South, became evident in July of that year at the Republican National Convention held in San Francisco, when 271 of 278 votes from delegations from the eleven states of the Old Confederacy supported Senator Goldwater's bid for the Republican presidential nomination. This high level of southern support was almost a third (30.7 per cent) of Goldwater's first–ballot strength, a proportion larger than that contributed by any other sector of the nation.[2]

Far more important than the role of the southern delegations at San Francisco, however, was the fact that Senator Goldwater became the first Republican presidential candidate to make victory in the South a major factor in his strategy for victory in the nation. This southern strategy was founded on three basic expectations.

First among these was the belief that 1964 would be a Republican year in the South. It was anticipated that the presidential Republicanism that had emerged with Dwight D. Eisenhower in 1952 and 1956, and which had continued at a lower level with Richard M. Nixon in 1960, would erupt full–blown with Senator Barry Goldwater as the Republican candidate in 1964.

The second expectation was that Goldwater would win the electoral votes of many midwestern and western states and that these, combined with the electoral votes of the southern states, would be enough to put him in the White House.

The third expectation was that many Republican candidates at the grassroots level would benefit from Goldwater's popularity and be carried into office with him.

These anticipated results of the southern strategy were proclaimed in the first pamphlet issued by the National Draft Goldwater Committee.

> Barry Goldwater will take all 128 electoral votes of the eleven Southern States! In 1964 Goldwater will give "the solid South" dramatic new meaning! *This is the key to Republican success!*

> In addition to sweeping the South, Goldwater will lead our party to a tremendous victory by carrying the dependable Republican states of the Midwest, Rocky Mountains, and Northern New England.

> The secret to Republican victory lies in the fact that Senator Goldwater can convert a past weakness of the Republican Party into great strength. He alone can tap this new reservoir of votes, not only for President, but also for control of Congress.[3]

The great expectations of the Goldwater high command for the southern strategy were crushed

by President Johnson's landslide victory. Senator
Goldwater failed to "take all 128 votes of the
eleven Southern States!" and yet even in defeat
his southern box score was indeed impressive: five
states, 47 electoral votes, 48.6 per cent of the
total vote.[4] This outcome compares favorably with
those of Eisenhower and Nixon. General Eisenhower had carried four states in 1952 and five
in 1956, for southern electoral–vote totals of 57
and 67, and total–vote percentages of 48.1 and
48.9—the last figure representing a plurality. In
1960, Vice–President Nixon had won only three
states, 33 electoral votes, and 46 per cent of the
total vote.

Thus, in terms of both states won and proportion of the total southern vote, Goldwater did better than Nixon, and about as well as Eisenhower
had done in his record–smashing performance of
1956. In southern electoral votes, Goldwater
failed to match Eisenhower's best showing, but
fared better than Nixon.

However, these southwide totals clearly do not
indicate of themselves certain important differences between the Goldwater outcome and the
Eisenhower and Nixon outcomes. These differences become apparent at the subregional level,
when election results in the Deep South are compared with those for the non–Deep South. (For
purposes of this study, the Deep South comprises

the states of Alabama, Georgia, Louisiana, Mississippi, and South Carolina; the non–Deep South
includes Arkansas, Florida, North Carolina, Tennessee, Texas, and Virginia.)

Eisenhower and Nixon both ran more than 10
percentage–points stronger in the non–Deep
South than in the Deep South. Moreover, the six
non–Deep South states provided Eisenhower with
majorities of their popular vote and Nixon with a
plurality. All of the electoral votes won by the
Republican Party in 1952 and 1960, plus 57 of
the 67 secured by Eisenhower in 1956, were contributed by states of the non–Deep South.

By contrast, the Republican proportion of the
presidential vote in the Deep South over this same
period never reached 40 per cent. The best showing by a Republican candidate was Eisenhower's
39.7 per cent in 1952. And the only Deep South
state to give its electoral votes to a Republican
presidential candidate in this century, prior to
1964, was Louisiana in 1956.

From the broad contours of 1964 election results at the subregional level, it is clear that Goldwater carried a different "South" than his
predecessors and that by so doing he caused what
appeared as a dramatic change in voting alignments. In the Deep South, the Goldwater candidacy enlisted the support of electoral majorities,
largely composed of the votes of Democrats, many

of whom were casting their ballots for a Republican presidential candidate for the first time in their lives. In the non–Deep South, on the other hand, the Goldwater candidacy had the effect of alienating voters in sufficient numbers to drop Goldwater below Nixon in percentage–point terms and, most importantly, to deny him the electoral votes of the six non–Deep South states in which his immediate predecessors had enjoyed a fair measure of success.

In short, change in voting preferences, rather than continuity, was outwardly the most visible component of the Goldwater outcome at the sub-regional level. It is this component of change that once again directs attention to the central question of southern politics, the development of a second party in the region, and to the most critical aspect of that development, the growth of the Republican Party within southern electorates.

The question of a second party for the South is susceptible to a number of interpretations in the light of the Goldwater outcome. It may well be, since Goldwater drew the disproportionate share of his strength from the subregion in which Eisenhower and Nixon had been least successful, that the election of 1964 was a deviating election for the South as a region, and that in future elections Republican candidates other than Goldwater will once again draw their heaviest support from

states of the non–Deep South. Conversely, it
might be supposed that the election of 1964
marked the conversion of the Deep South into a
reliably Republican subregion.

But these and similar speculations, if based
solely on gross election results drawn from the
South and its subregions, must be regarded as
tentative at best. Data of such generality do not
provide adequate empirical support for any but
the most cautiously developed propositions. Indeed, southwide and subregional data raise a
variety of specific questions about the condition
of the Republican Party in the South—questions
that are not readily answerable through analysis
of gross results alone. For example, in precisely
what sectors and subregions of the South were
traditional voting patterns disrupted by the Goldwater outcome, and what exactly was the nature
of the disruption? Where, in other words, was
there more evidence of change than of continuity?
What was the magnitude of change? What categories of the electorate were principally responsi-
ble for it? Conversely, to what extent was there
evidence of continuity—where, and among what
categories of the electorate?

Aside from their intrinsic historical interest,
these and similar questions about the continuity
and change exhibited in southern presidential voting behavior should be considered when any

attempt is made to discern the apparent direction of southern politics, especially with respect to the prospects–for–growth of the Republican Party in the region.

The present work is based on official election returns and the assumption that systematic analysis of these aggregate data for a number of presidential elections permits the identification of continuities and changes in mass voting behavior over a period of time. Suppose it could be shown, for example, that Senator Goldwater ran strongest in parts of the South where Eisenhower and Nixon also had achieved a high degree of success. Considering the many differences, real or imagined, among these Republicans, their all having done well in the same sectors of the South, and among like categories of voters, might well be interpreted as evidence of the development of a stable presidential Republicanism. If, on the other hand, systematic analyses of aggregate data revealed dissimilar patterns of support for Eisenhower, Nixon, and Goldwater, then the stability of southern presidential Republicanism might seem more problematical. There is, of course, the possibility of a mixed result, one in which the voting patterns display significant elements of both continuity and change.

In using election returns as basic data, it is necessary to keep in mind their analytical limitations and strengths. Analyses based on aggregate data often shed considerable light on macro–political behavior, but are much less illuminating in explaining micro–political behavior, that is, in identifying and explaining the nature and causes of individual political behavior. The election results from even the smallest of political subdivisions, such as precincts or wards, allow only crude inferences about motivating forces at work upon the individual voter. Gross determinations of the components of the electoral decision (e.g., candidates and issues, and their import for particular categories of voters) are meaningful and perhaps even sufficient for understanding some aspects of political behavior. In general, however, aggregate data are of very limited usefulness in investigating the psychology of the individual in the voting booth. A voter might well support Eisenhower, Nixon, and Goldwater, but perhaps for different reasons, none of which could be verified by analysis of aggregative data alone.

Then, too, while the analysis of aggregate data may reveal secular (long term) and cyclical (short term) movements in voting behavior over the years, analyses of this type usually result in only rough estimations of the extent to which such movements are attributable to particular categories of voters. For example, shifts of voters from one party to another may be detected in the election returns from small subdivisions, but on the basis of aggregate data alone it is difficult to measure precisely the net effect of changes in political allegiance.[5]

Despite these and other limitations on their use, aggregate data are of significant value to the political analyst because of their completeness, their relative freedom from error, their ease of replication, and their availability over long periods of time.[6] All of these advantages are particularly important to the individual researcher, who may test and perhaps even elaborate the findings of aggregative studies, ordinarily with a minimum expenditure of time and money.

In addition to relying upon aggregative data, this study includes in its structural framework a four–way division of the South, its subregions, and its states, somewhat along the lines suggested by James Burns when he wrote that "the future of Southern politics turns mainly on developments in these critical areas—the Democratic black–belt, the cities and industrialized areas, and to a lesser extent the mountain Republican districts".[7] To the three sectors suggested by Burns may be added a fourth—the non–metropolitan South. Each sector consists of counties that have certain definable features in common, irrespective of state boundaries, as follows:

1. *The Traditionally–Republican South* includes counties in which Republican presidential candidates received a minimum of 35 per cent of the vote in three–fourths of the presidential elections from 1900 to 1948 (the election of 1912 was excluded). A total of 141 counties fit this definition. As expected, most of them are in the states of North Carolina, Tennessee, and Virginia. The others are in Alabama, Arkansas, Georgia, and Texas. Four traditionally–Republican counties have cities of 50,000 population but are included here rather than in the metropolitan sector. These are Forsyth County (Winston-Salem) and Guilford County (Greensboro), both in North Carolina; and Hamilton County (Chattanooga) and Knox County (Knoxville), both in Tennessee.

2. *The Metropolitan South* comprises the fifty-six counties that are listed in the Census of 1960 as having cities of 50,000 population, plus Virginia's eight independent cities.

3. *The Black–Belt South* consists of the 138 counties that had non–white majorities in 1960. About three–fourths of them are in the five Deep South states of Alabama, Georgia, Louisiana, Mississippi, and South Carolina.

4. *The Non–Metropolitan South* consists of the remaining counties.

What follows is an examination of the pattern of the Republican presidential vote of 1964 in relationship to pre–1964 voting alignments in these four sectors—first in terms of the South as a region (Chapter 1) and then at the subregional and statewide levels (Chapters 2 and 3).

CHAPTER I

Voting Patterns in the Eleven Southern States, 1920–1964

AT THE SOUTHWIDE LEVEL, THE GOLD-water candidacy brought about an apparent reversal of very long–standing, presidential voting alignments. In terms of the four sectors used in the present analysis, Goldwater did best in the black–belt, least well in the cities (see Figure 1). There is no precedent anywhere in the electoral data of the last four decades for either the arrangement

Figure 1. Presidential Republicanism in the South, 1920–1964: GOP percentages of the total presidential vote in the metropolitan, non–metropolitan, black–belt, and traditionally Republican sectors of the South and in the Nation.

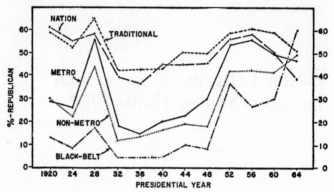

of the Goldwater percentages by sector or the emergence of black–belt presidential Republicanism on such a grand scale.

Republican presidential candidates from 1920 to 1960, beginning with Warren G. Harding and continuing through Richard Nixon, have secured their best percentages in the traditionally–Republican counties. Indeed, in all but two of the presidential elections since 1920 Republican nominees have done better in traditionally–Republican southern counties than they have in the nation as a whole.

Aside from this "traditional . . . Republicanism", found in seven of the southern states, probably the best known feature of presidential Republicanism in the South has been the greater willingness of metropolitan electorates, as compared to voters in the non–metropolitan sector, to support Republican nominees. Republicans from Coolidge to Nixon have received significantly higher percentages of the vote in the urban South than in its non–urban and black–belt sectors. And, in the 1950's the Republican proportion of the southwide metropolitan presidential vote approached the levels of Republicanism in the traditionally–Republican counties and in the nation, whereas the party's non–metropolitan and black–belt percentages lagged considerably behind.

In sum, then, in each of the eleven presidential elections from 1920 through 1960, Republican vote divisions in each sector followed a distinct pattern, ranging downward in magnitude from the traditionally–Republican counties, to the metropolitan and non–metropolitan sectors, to the black–belt. In 1964, however, this pattern was replaced by one in which the Republican candidate was most successful in the black–belt.

If the surge of Republican balloting in the black–belt was the most noteworthy component of the Goldwater outcome in the South, it was also its most easily predictable feature, given the ways in which Goldwater's southern strategy was implemented during the campaign. Neither Dewey nor

Eisenhower nor Nixon had adopted a strategy
congenial to the many black–belt white voters for
whom the most important issue—the all–important issue—was race. Thus, prior to 1964 the
absence of a Republican alternative on the race
issue, coupled with the abandonment by the
Democratic presidential party of its role as the
party of the southern white man, had served to
neutralize the issue insofar as competition between
the major parties was concerned. To many southerners, neither party was "right on race".

In 1948, left without a major party alternative
with respect to this issue, the majority of white
voters in the black–belt defected from the Democratic Party to the States' Rights Party. (In the
context of post–World War II southern politics,
and throughout this book, the so–called issue of
"states rights" signifies the "race" issue—or issues
—as it was conceived from a more–or–less traditionally segregationist, or white–supremacist,
viewpoint.) The States' Rights Party may also
have made inroads into presidential Republicanism, since the proportion of Dewey's vote in the
black–belt sector was smaller in 1948 than in
1944. Be that as it may, in 1952 the black–belt
participated in the general surge of enthusiasm for
Eisenhower, but apparently for different reasons
than those that led many other southerners to
presidential Republicanism. For, while Eisen-

hower continued to improve his showing in other sectors of the South, black–belt enthusiasm for him dropped–off sharply in 1956, except in black–belt counties having many Negro voters. But in 1960, when southern presidential Republicanism generally subsided from the high southwide levels of 1956, it once again increased in the black–belt.[1]

Intentionally or not, in 1964 the Republican presidential party, for the first time in history, played the role of the "traditional" party of the South—with the startling results already mentioned. What had long been the bedrock of the Democratic Party in the subregion in 1964 produced a GOP percentage of 59.6—a gain of some 30 percentage–points over Nixon's black–belt showing. While Eisenhower's advance from Dewey had matched almost exactly the magnitude of Goldwater's black–belt gain over Nixon, neither Eisenhower nor Nixon had received as much as 40 per cent of this vote. Their best showing in the sector was Eisenhower's 37 per cent in 1952.

In sectors other than the black–belt there has been a good deal of variability in the Republican vote since 1920. As is shown in Figure 1, before 1948 presidential Republicanism displayed its greatest amount of change in sectors other than the black–belt. For much of this earlier period the Democratic presidential party was "right" on the race issue, and as a result black–belt presidential

Republicanism remained more rumor than reality, rising above the 20 per cent mark only once, in 1928, a year in which presidential Republicanism also increased sharply in other sectors of the region. But this early Republican surge was followed by a rapid decline to the low point of 1932 in the countryside and traditionally–Republican areas, and the low point of 1936 in the cities.

In the metropolitan sector, presidential Republicanism gained slowly but steadily from 1940 through 1948, increased spectacularly with the candidacy of Dwight D. Eisenhower in 1952 and gained a bit more in 1956, and suffered only a modest decline with Nixon in 1960. Non–metropolitan presidential Republicanism followed a somewhat similar course, except for slight losses in 1948 and 1956 and a small gain registered in 1960.

Traditional–Republicanism continued at a higher level than the other varieties and, not unexpectedly, displayed considerably less variance. The hard core of this vote was probably struck in the 1930's and in 1940, when traditional–Republicanism leveled–off at just over 40 per cent. Subsequently, this traditional–Republicanism of the mountain counties increased in 1944, declined in 1948, reached majority proportions greater than 55 per cent in 1952 and 60 per cent in 1956, and declined slightly to 58 per cent in 1960.

The declines in the presidential Republicanism of traditionally–Republican and metropolitan counties, and the rise in the non–metropolitan sector, all of which occurred from 1956 to 1960, continued with Goldwater in 1964. However, Goldwater's gain in the non–metropolitan sector of 7 percentage–points, while relatively substantial, gave him a total of only 48.8 per cent of the total vote. His heaviest loss was sustained in the traditionally–Republican sector, where the Republican proportion of the vote fell from the 58.8 per cent of 1960 to 50.4 in 1964, a decline of 8.4 percentage–points.

Even with this decline, however, Goldwater did receive an over–all majority in the traditionally–Republican counties, whereas he did not do so in the cities. The metropolitan loss amounted to less than one–half of the decline in the traditionally–Republican sector, but it was of sufficient magnitude to deny Goldwater an urban majority. Not since Dewey (1948) had a Republican presidential nominee failed to carry the South's cities. Eisenhower received majorities of the urban vote in both 1952 and 1956, and Nixon received a plurality in 1960. Both of these Republicans ran appreciably stronger in the cities than they did in the other sectors of the non–traditionally–Republican South. Goldwater, in contrast, not only lost the metropolitan South, but proved to be less pop-

ular in the cities than he was in the non–metropolitan sector. Though the spread between his votes
in these two sectors was a mere 2 percentage–
points, one must go back to 1920 and Warren
Gamaliel Harding to find a Republican standard–
bearer who, like Goldwater, did better in the non–
metropolitan South than in the cities.

CHAPTER II

Voting Patterns
in the Deep South

THE SOUTHERN STRATEGY OF THE RE-
publicans yielded the desired result in the Deep
South. Senator Goldwater swept the subregion
and each of its sectors. He doubled Nixon's black–
belt and non–metropolitan percentages, and improved upon Nixon's showing by fully 15 percentage–points in the cities, and by 7 percentage–
points in traditionally–Republican domain. The

net effect of these shifts to Goldwater was to give him a whopping majority in the black–belt, plus substantial majorities in other sectors, all of which clustered around 60 per cent.

The most dramatic component of the Goldwater outcome in the Deep South was—change. Whereas both Eisenhower and Nixon had been stronger in the cities and traditionally–Republican counties than they were in the black–belt, Goldwater's greatest success was in the black–belt. With Goldwater as the Republican standard–bearer, the voting alignments characteristic of the Eisenhower–Nixon period came to an end. Indeed, the Republican candidate of 1964 came close to turning the Eisenhower–Nixon voting patterns upside down and, in point of fact, the distribution of the Goldwater vote within the Deep South is related inversely to that of Eisenhower in 1956. To unearth a parallel to the Goldwater outcome, it is necessary to refer to the distribution of Democratic percentages in elections prior to 1948.

From James Cox in 1920 to Franklin D. Roosevelt's 1944 campaign, the Democratic vote reached its high point in the black–belt sector, and then tailed–off to lower, but still very substantial proportions in the non–metropolitan, metropolitan, and traditionally–Republican sectors, usually in that order. For most of the period bracketed by Cox and Roosevelt, the Democratic presidential party was "safe" on the race issue. However, in 1948 when the Democratic presidential party began to integrate the wishes and aspirations of Negro voters into its platform, Deep–South whites, and especially those in the black–belt, began to desert the Democratic Party. In that year four of the non–Deep South states and all of their black–belts defected to the States' Rights Party. In 1952, however, the Deep South was caught up in the general drift of sentiment for Eisenhower, and in all sectors, including the black–belt, presidential Republicanism rose above its 1948 level by upwards of 20 percentage–points. From Eisenhower to Nixon, the Republican vote outside the black–belt exhibited only light to moderate variations. Black–belt presidential Republicanism, however, fluctuated widely from 41.9 per cent in 1952 to 23.9 in 1956 to 32.3 per cent in the year 1960 (see Table 1).

The vicissitudes of black–belt voting behavior in 1948 and after reflected this electorate's search

TABLE 1: Presidential Republicanism in the Deep South, 1952–1964

Sector	Gold- water	Nixon	Eisenhower 1956	Eisenhower 1952	Gain 1960–64
Traditional	59.6	52.0	53.5	46.2	7.6
Metropolitan	60.2	44.4	48.6	47.8	15.8
Non–Metropolitan	61.6	30.9	33.1	34.4	30.9
Black–Belt	72.7	32.3	23.9	41.9	40.4

for a palatable racial alternative at the presidential
level. Race was also undoubtedly of concern to
most white voters elsewhere in the Deep South,
but many of them, unlike their neighbors in the
black–belt sector, were unwilling to support a
third party on racial grounds alone. The political
stimulus that might have activated their racial
anxieties was missing from the quadrennial contests of the 1950's and 1960, inasmuch as both
major presidential parties had refused to embrace
the cause of the southern white. For this reason,
it seems highly unlikely that race was the critical
factor in determining the aggregate vote division
for and against Nixon or Eisenhower. But as
racial tensions increased in the Deep South early
in the 1960's, and dissatisfaction with the implementation of civil rights policies by Presidents
Kennedy and Johnson swept southern white electorates, the race issue became easily exploitable in
state and local contests and more susceptible to
exploitation at the presidential level, when and if
a candidate should emerge as an avowed cham-
pion of southern "states' rights". Goldwater was
that candidate. And, when he directed his "states'
rights" appeal at the South, white electorates in
the Deep South responded much as their grand-
fathers would have. They voted for what they
perceived to be the "candidate of the southern
white man".

Empirical support for this view of the impact of race upon Deep–South electorates can be found in statewide voting patterns. Of initial interest are the outcomes of the senatorial elections of 1962, in which race first emerged as a positive Republican influence in grassroots interparty competition. Republican candidates Martin in Alabama, O'Hearn in Louisiana, and Workman in South Carolina were dedicated Goldwater supporters, who based their campaigns, at least in part, on traditional southern "states' rights", and who benefited from the burgeoning dissatisfaction of Deep–South white electorates with the national Democratic Party—a condition intensified during the campaigns by Federal involvement in the integration of the University of Mississippi.

While the votes garnered by these Republicans ranged downward from Martin's near miss of 49.1 per cent in Alabama, through Workman's 42.8 per cent in South Carolina, to O'Hearn's 24.4 per cent in Louisiana, the voting patterns and per-centage–point gains relative to their most immediate predecessors served as harbingers of the Goldwater outcome in the Deep South. Each of these Republicans profited from a surge of votes which, though it varied considerably in amplitude, had the effect of producing larger Republican percentages in the black–belt than non–metropolitan sectors of all three states, and which established the black–belt as the "most Republican" sector in both Alabama and Louisiana. This rapid acceleration of Republican strength at the grassroots also resulted in the pattern of percentage–point gains that was to be replicated by Senator Goldwater at the southwide and sub-regional levels and in four of the five Deep–South states. These pre–Goldwater voting alignments are displayed in Table 2.

TABLE 2: Grassroots Republicanism in the Deep South, 1962—*Republican Proportions of the Senatorial Vote in Alabama, Louisiana, and South Carolina*

Sector	Alabama		Louisiana		South Carolina	
	% Rep.	%–point Gain '60–'62	% Rep.	%–point Gain '60–'62	% Rep.	%–point Gain '60–'62
Traditional	47.3	5.3				
Metropolitan	52.6	20.2	26.6	3.3	52.95	19.3
Non–Metro-politan	45.0	19.2	21.8	4.0	37.01	23.8
Black–Belt	52.8	29.4	32.9	17.3	40.9	33.3

The racial dimension of the Goldwater outcome in the Deep South emerges quite clearly from statewide voting patterns set out in Table 3 and from the Republican shifts, 1960 to 1964, displayed in Table 4.

The most conspicuous feature emerging from the data of Table 3 was the surge of Republicans, of which the most dramatic aspect was the out-

TABLE 3: Goldwater in the Deep South States

Sector	Ala.	Ga.	La.	Miss.	S. C.
Traditional	63.9	48.9			
Metropolitan	68.9	52.2	57.6	87.9	59.8 (54.6)[b]
Non–Metropolitan	70.1	54.2	55.6 (64.4)[a]	86.2	57.2 (58.7)[b]
Black–Belt	75.4	61.4	67.5 (79.8)[a]	90.1	64.5 (68.5)[b]

[a] Percentage Republican when Roman Catholic counties are omitted.

[b] Percentage Republican when counties having 20 per cent or more non–white registration are omitted.

TABLE 4: Goldwater and Nixon in the Deep South States—*Republican Percentage–Point Gains, Loss in Sectors of the Five Deep South States, 1960–1964*

Sector	Percentage–Point Gain or Loss, 1960–1964				
	Ala.	Ga.	La.	Miss.	S. C.
Traditional	+13.6	− 7.7			
Metro	+20.6	+ 2.5	+24.6	+49.7	− 3.4
Non–Metro	+35.8	+22.1	+30.3	+62.8	+15.8
Black–Belt	+36.1	+37.4	+39.8	+67.5	+10.3

break of black–belt presidential Republicanism on a grand scale. In each state Goldwater's top percentage was recorded in the black–belt sector. He received more than six of ten black–belt votes in Georgia, Louisiana, and South Carolina; more than seven of ten in black–belt Alabama, and almost unanimous support from this electorate in Mississippi. But Goldwater's popularity (and presumably the racial component of his appeal) was not confined to black–belt electorates. Of the subregion's seventeen sectors, Goldwater carried all but one, traditionally–Republican Georgia, and in only two, metropolitan and non–metropolitan Georgia, did his share of the vote dip below 55 per cent.

The extent of the Goldwater appeal was evident also in the magnitude of the Republican shifts from 1960 to 1964, as shown in Table 4. These favored Goldwater by at least 10 percentage–points in fourteen sectors. In one of them, metropolitan Georgia, he improved on Nixon's 1960 showing by 2.5 percentage–points, and he dropped behind Nixon in only two sectors, traditionally–Republican Georgia and metropolitan South Carolina. In four of the Deep South states the pattern of Republican gains is the familiar one, already apparent at the southwide and subregional levels and in the 1962 senatorial contests.

South Carolina was the exception. In this Deep South state the Republican shift was not only of considerably greater magnitude in the non–metropolitan sector than it was in the black–belt, but Goldwater lost ground to Nixon in the cities. These gains and losses may possibly be explained, at least in part, by the fact of South Carolina's having experienced a resurgence of presidential Republicanism four years in advance of other

Deep South states. In 1960, Nixon's vote reached majority proportions in South Carolina's metropolitan and black–belt sectors. He received almost two-thirds of the metropolitan vote (63.2 per cent), and carried fifteen of the then twenty–one black–belt counties with a sectorwide percentage of 54.2. This figure outstripped by more than 17 percentage–points his showing in any other portion of the Deep South black–belt sector. The resurgence of Republicans in South Carolina in 1960 apparently had the effect of placing a ceiling on the possible magnitude of future pro–Republican shifts in that state's metropolitan and black–belt sectors.

As a consequence of the Republican shifts within the Deep South states from 1960 to 1964, voting patterns in Alabama and Georgia paralleled those at the regional and subregional levels. That is, the Goldwater vote reached its highest level in the black–belt, and then declined in amplitude from the non–metropolitan sector to the cities and traditionally–Republican counties. Louisiana and Mississippi joined South Carolina as states in which the Republican presidential nominee did better in the cities than the countryside. However, these deviations from regional and subregional norms can be made to "disappear" from the South Carolina outcome by omitting from consideration the data from each county in each sector in which more than 20 per cent of the electorate was Negro.[1] The deviations can also be made to disappear from the Louisiana outcome by omitting from consideration parishes with Roman Catholic majorities in the non–metropolitan and black–belt sectors—the only sectors having such parishes.[2] (One might anticipate a similar result in Mississippi if registration data for race were available from that state.)

The obvious inference to be drawn from this treatment of the data is, of course, that Catholics in Louisiana and Negro voters in South Carolina were heavily in favor of the Democratic presidential candidate in 1964. This was, in fact, the case. Louisiana's eighteen Catholic parishes, which had supported Eisenhower in 1956 but returned to the Democratic Party to vote for Kennedy in 1960, continued their support of Democratic candidates in 1964.[3] The Johnson–Humphrey ticket received 53.0 per cent of this vote, a proportion no doubt augmented by a heavy non–white registration. (Negro voting behavior in the Deep South is discussed elsewhere in this chapter.)

A final conclusion which emerges from a reading of Tables 3 and 4 is that voting patterns within three Deep South states diverged markedly from alignments characteristic of 1952, 1956, and 1960. In Alabama, Georgia, and Mississippi,

Nixon and Eisenhower found the cities to be more reliably Republican than either the black–belt or the countryside. Indeed, this had been the shape of the outcome in Georgia since 1948, in Alabama since 1940, and in Mississippi since 1936. This also had been the pattern in Louisiana from 1940 and in South Carolina from 1936, though in these states the Goldwater result did not diverge from the Nixon outcome as markedly as it did elsewhere in the Deep South.

Indications of continuity as well as change in the Goldwater vote at the statewide level become clearer when counties of each Deep South state are ranked in descending order according to the size of their Republican percentages in the last three presidential elections (1956, 1960, and 1964) and the rankings are correlated. The coefficients of correlation are set out below.

	R, 1956–60	R, 1960–64
Alabama	.88	.06
Georgia	.80	.06
Louisiana	.04	.64
Mississippi	.66	−.33
South Carolina	.30	.73

The first point to be made on the basis of these correlations is that they support the proposition that Goldwater disrupted previously well–defined voting patterns in three of the Deep South states.

In Alabama and Georgia, the magnitude of the coefficients suggests a close relationship between Eisenhower and Nixon but little or none between Nixon and Goldwater. A coefficient of lesser but nonetheless significant proportions links Eisenhower and Nixon in Mississippi, while a negative coefficient gives emphasis to the sharp reversal of Nixon by Goldwater in this state. In Louisiana and South Carolina, on the other hand, a different set of relationships prevails. In South Carolina the relationship between Eisenhower and Nixon is slight and in Louisiana nil. There is, however, a rather close correspondence between Nixon and Goldwater in both of these states. This last finding deserves more detailed attention.

It must be emphasized at the outset that the coefficient linking Nixon and Goldwater in Louisiana should not be interpreted to mean that their votes were related in other than the most general way. Nixon received only 28 per cent of the statewide total vote. Goldwater doubled that proportion with a statewide majority of 55 per cent. Nixon received the disproportionate share of his vote from the Protestant parishes, most of which are situated in the northern–half of the state. But, while Nixon ran ahead of Kennedy in parishes with heavy concentrations of Protestant voters, more than one in every four voters in this elector-

ate had drifted–off to support a "States' Rights
Party". Goldwater, like Nixon, was strongest in
Protestant north–Louisiana.[4] However, unlike
Nixon, Goldwater did not have to share his potential vote with a third party. Implementation of
Goldwater's "southern strategy" removed the need
for a third party in 1964, with the result that
he received not only his predecessor's base vote
but also the votes of persons who had supported
Kennedy but were repelled by Johnson, plus the
votes of persons who had rejected both major
parties in 1960—that is, persons who had supported the "States' " Rights Party—but who considered Goldwater an acceptable alternative to
Johnson in 1964. A States' Rights–into–Republican vote was visible not only in Louisiana, but also
in Mississippi. This characteristic of the Goldwater outcome in the Deep South is reflected in the
coefficients that result from the correlation of
Goldwater and third party votes in these two
states. For Louisiana R is .82; for Mississippi R
is .73.

For indications of a States' Rights–into–Republican vote in South Carolina, the only other Deep
South state which has had a significant third
party movement since 1948, one must refer to the
election of 1956, when an independent slate of
presidential electors, uncommitted to any partic-

ular candidate, polled about three out of every ten votes and carried twenty–one of the state's forty–six counties. Four years later, electorates in sixteen of the twenty–one counties gave Nixon majorities of their votes, and in the five remaining counties he came close to winning, with between 48.0 and 49.9 per cent of the vote in four, 45.6 per cent in one. Moreover, the correlation of the Republican vote of 1960 and the third party of 1956 yielded a positive coefficient of .66. A positive coefficient of equivalent amplitude, .67, was produced by relating the Goldwater and independent–elector outcomes. Thus, South Carolina experienced a States' Rights–into–Republican vote prior to the other Deep South states.

This discussion of over–lapping support for "states' rights" parties and the Republican Party in three Deep South states makes no pretense at having exhausted the subject. Indeed, the most obvious possibility for overlap has yet to be developed, except in the broadest outline. Taken at its face value, the Goldwater outcome appears more nearly like that of the States' Rights Party of 1948 than other recent electoral outcomes in the subregion. We have sought to test for a relationship between 1964 and 1948 by correlating the Goldwater and Thurmond votes within each of the Deep South states, with the following results:

	R, 1948–64	
Alabama	.52	(.57)
Georgia	.57	(.63)
Louisiana	.36	(.53)
Mississippi	.71	
South Carolina	.76	(.80)

Considering the dynamic changes which have been underway in the electoral context of the Deep South since 1948, including basic changes in the size and composition of its electorate, the coefficients relating 1964 and 1948 reached levels of some significance in four states, and particularly in two of them, Mississippi and South Carolina. At first glance, there appears to have been little relationship between the Goldwater and Thurmond votes in Louisiana. To some extent, the absence of a correlation in this state may be attributed to the shifting preferences of its Roman Catholic electorate. These voters had been considerably less enthusiastic for Goldwater than for Thurmond. Thus, when the eighteen parishes with Catholic majorities are removed from the data, R in Louisiana increases to .53, indicating both the significance of Roman Catholicism and the fact that variables other than Catholic concentration account for much of the differential in the Republican and "states' rights" votes. One possible explanatory variable is non–white registration.[5] But when the parishes having Negro registrants in excess of 20 per cent of total registration are removed from the data, the coefficient rises only slightly to .55. Similarly, R is amplified by only a small degree when counties having heavy Negro registration are taken out of the election returns from Alabama, Georgia, and South Carolina.

Though we have undertaken what is admittedly little more than a preliminary analysis of these data, from the standpoint of understanding the Goldwater outcome it is surely of the utmost significance that coefficients linking Goldwater to Thurmond are appreciably stronger than those relating Goldwater to Nixon in Alabama, Georgia, and Mississippi, and that in South Carolina the coefficients relating the two sets of outcomes are of equivalent value. All of these relationships point to the racial component of the Goldwater outcome in the Deep South.

In focusing on overlap between support for Goldwater and "states' rights" parties, we have been dealing with those white electorates in which racial concern is of the highest intensity. Yet, up to this point we have referred to the object of their concern, the Negro and to his role in shaping the Goldwater outcome, only vaguely and then usually by implication.

It is scarcely news to report that a greater proportion of Negroes had registered to vote in 1964 than in any previous quadrennial election. Registration data made available for four Deep South states by the U. S. Commission on Civil Rights, but which in three states consist of estimates rather than official tabulations, places the Negro proportion of the subregion's total registration—Mississippi excluded—at 12.1 per cent. It was not at all surprising that this segment of the southern electorate was unable to build up any real enthusiasm for the Republican nominee of 1964—and not merely because Republican leaders in the Deep South evinced little if any sustained interest in cultivating the Negro voter. Goldwater's vote against the Civil Rights Act of 1964 and his continuing emphasis of "states' rights" was nicely fitted to his "southern strategy" and assured him of strong support from white voters in the Deep South. From the standpoint of non–white voters, however, Goldwater's actions and words made him unacceptible. The result of Goldwater's southern strategy was the almost complete withdrawal of Negroes from the Republican presidential party.

In Table 5 the Goldwater and Nixon votes have been summed and expressed as percentages at intervals of counties of four Deep South states, grouped according to the non–white proportion of their registered electorate. When the data are arranged in this way, an inverse relationship appears between the level of non–white registration and the magnitude of both Goldwater's percentages of the vote and his percentage–point gains relative to Nixon. There was no relationship in 1960, although percentage–point gains computed from that year to 1964 relate to the classification, except at the 30–39 interval, where the Republican increase was larger than at the 20–29 interval. A more precise relationship exists between the Goldwater vote and non–white registration when the black–belt counties are segregated from the classification and considered separately as in Table 6. The commanding feature of these data is the very pronounced relationship between the level of Goldwater's support and the Republican shifts from 1960 and non–white registration. The distances shown between his vote and gains at the extremes of the classification, which exceed 40 when measured in percentage–points, are clear

TABLE 5: Republican Proportions of the Total Presidential Vote in Counties of Four Deep South States Classified by Percentage Negro of Total Registration

Negro Percentage of Total Registration	Number of Counties	Per Cent Republican 1964	Per Cent Republican 1960	%–Point Gain 1960–1964
40 or more	5	35.9	25.1	10.8
30–39	13	50.7	33.1	17.6
20–29	40	53.3	42.8	10.5
10–19	109	59.3	38.4	20.9
0–9	169	61.9	34.3	27.6

TABLE 6: Republican Proportion of the Total Presidential Vote in Black–Belt Counties of Four Deep South States Classified by Percentage Negro of Total Registration

Negro Percentage of Total Registration	Number of Counties	Per Cent Republican 1964	1960	%–Point Gain 1960–1964
40 or more	4	34.9	21.8	13.1
30–39	5	51.4	38.2	13.2
20–29	11	59.3	40.98	18.3
10–19	23	66.5	40.3	26.2
1–9	26	77.97	32.2	45.8
Under 1	2	87.7	32.5	55.2

Data source for non–white registration: *United States Commission on Civil Rights*, Information Center, Washington, D.C., March 19, 1965. The registration figures for counties of Alabama, Georgia, and South Carolina are estimates.

indications that for most white voters Goldwater was a highly attractive candidate, whereas he was quite the opposite for most Negro voters.

It should be apparent from the foregoing that the Goldwater candidacy accelerated, increased, and brought to a culmination the growing Negro alienation from the Republican Party that was discernible in the Nixon outcome in 1960. If, however, there is need for additional evidence of a Negro shift, one need only turn to the cities, for nowhere in the Deep South was the withdrawal of Negroes from the Republican Party more dramatically visible than in the metropol-

itan sector. As a source of data for the voting
behavior of urban Negroes we have available
election returns from twenty–three of the pre-
dominantly non–white precincts and wards that
were used by the National Broadcasting Company in its "Operation Ballot". In these Negro
"Tag" precincts, the vote division for Goldwater
was a minuscule 1.6 per cent, representing a
drop–off from Nixon of 51.8 percentage–points.[6]

The depth of Negro disenchantment with the
Republican presidential party can be seen best in
metropolitan Alabama. In this state the Negro
voter faced a hard choice. He could vote for
Senator Goldwater or he could vote for a slate of
so–called "independent electors" who had won
possession of the Democratic label on the general
election ballot by defeating a slate of "loyalist
electors" in the Democratic primary. At the time
of the primary, in May, the "independent electors" were pledged to Governor George Wallace.
By November, however, there was considerable
uncertainty as to whom they might support in the
electoral college, Wallace having withdrawn as a
candidate. The only relatively–certain possibility
seemed to be none of the "independent electors"
would cast his ballot for the nominees of either
major presidential party. Beyond these negative
commitments, however, the question of what the
"independent electors" might actually do was a

matter for conjecture—of which there was a good deal. From the point of view of most Negro voters, neither possible choice—to vote Republican or for the "independent electors"—inspired even qualified enthusiasm. On election day, with what must have been mixed emotions, overwhelming numbers of Alabama's Negroes voted for the "independent electors".

Birmingham has two election districts with levels of non–white occupancy in excess of 96 per cent (1960 U. S. housing census), in both of which Negroes constituted 99 per cent of the registered electorate in 1964. In these districts Goldwater polled only 39 votes out of 3,819 cast with the remainder going to the "independent electors". (In recent elections, only Public Safety Commissioner Eugene "Bull" Connor had managed a vote of equivalently low proportions in these districts.) In other Alabama cities for which election returns at the ward or precinct levels are available, the direction of the Negro vote was much the same as it was in Birmingham. In Mobile, for example, the ward with the highest proportion of Negroes produced 17 votes for Goldwater, 2,032 for the independent electors. In Montgomery the Negro ward divided by a vote of 1,013 to 595 in favor of the independent electors. In Gadsden, the Negro precinct went to the independent electors by a vote of 316 to 26. Though

there were variations in the relative magnitude of
the Goldwater and independent–elector votes in
the Negro precincts and wards, many could be
attributed to different levels of non–white population. Thus, according to the 1960 U. S. housing
census, Negroes occupied 99 per cent of the
dwelling units in the Mobile ward but less than 90
per cent in the Gadsden precinct, and no more
than 75 per cent in the Montgomery ward. Verily,
as one Negro leader is reported to have predicted:
"Every registered Negro [went] to the polls and
[voted] for Johnson." [7]

An equally significant component of the Goldwater outcome in Deep South cities was the voting
pattern in the predominately white wards and precincts. A well–established generalization in the lit-
erature of American political behavior is that
urbanization modifies political sectionalism. For
decades, the most often–voiced expectation for
the future of southern politics was that political
change would come first in the cities. But even in
metropolitan environments political changes tend
to lag behind social and economic developments,
and such developments usually do not become
politically significant until such time as they are
linked to political alternatives (parties, candidates) that are related to differences in social
attributes (status, race, etc.) as, for example, the
competing domestic social welfare policies of the

Democratic and Republican presidential parties
have been related to class status since the 1930's
in the metropolitan South.[8] Urbanization and related forces, as V. O. Key pointed out, have "built
within the southern cities neighborhoods of upper–
income proprietors and managers with an economic base largely independent of the region's
old agrarian interests. The new business classes,
like the old business classes of the North, [have]
had little enthusiasm for the New Deal and Fair
Deal." [9] Repelled by the social welfare activity
generated by the Roosevelt and Truman adminis-
trations, many upper–status whites have turned to
the Republican Party as the more sufferable
alternative.

Information about the voting behavior of the
southern city dweller prior to the 1950's is not
abundant, but that which is available supports the
notion that upper–status southern urbanites have
long been behaving politically like their counterparts elsewhere in the country. For example,
Charles Farris found upper–income enthusiasm
for a Republican presidential candidate in Jack-
sonville, Florida, as far back in time as Hoover
in 1932. Samuel Lubell uncovered upper–income
support for Alf Landon in Houston in 1936. And
the present writer found that in Asheville, North
Carolina, Thomas E. Dewey ran best (1948) in
the more prosperous precincts.[10]

The expectation that political change occurs most readily in cities was confirmed by the metropolitan voting divisions of the Eisenhower–Nixon period. Working with aggregate data drawn from the urban South, Donald S. Strong demonstrated that upper– and middle–status whites responded to Eisenhower at markedly high levels of support in 1952 and again in 1956, and the present writer found that these same voters gave Nixon exceptionally high levels of support in 1960.[11]

Class bias in the southern presidential vote was also detectable in survey data.[12] The Survey Research Center at the University of Michigan found a movement toward a positive correlation of class status and party identification in the South for the years from 1952 to 1960. Also of considerable import was the Center's finding that when status polarization (i.e., the relationship between class status and the vote) was correlated with industrialization, a positive coefficient emerged in southern industrial counties, but negative coefficients resulted in both an intermediate category and a rural category.[13] In sum, aggregationists and survey researchers have both interpreted the Republican emergence in southern urban areas as the most persuasive evidence yet uncovered of the dissolution of the multi–class composition of the region's presidential vote and the appearance of voting alignments more nearly congruent with class stratifications. But whether the Republican vote would continue to parallel the socio–economic differentials among racially–aroused metropolitan electorates was one of the leading questions to be answered by the Goldwater outcome.

Some indication of the possible effect of race upon metropolitan electorates can be discerned in the vote for Republican senatorial candidate James Martin in Birmingham, Alabama, in 1962. At that time it was generally conceded that, of all cities in the Deep South, Birmingham represented a hard core of resistance to change in the racial status quo, a civic condition that in 1962 was personified in the words and deeds of Public Safety Commissioner Eugene "Bull" Connor. In an electoral contest in which race was the principal issue, Martin received 54 per cent of the city's total vote, only 3 percentage–points below Nixon's showing two years earlier. Within Birmingham, Martin's percentages at each level of a classification of predominately–white districts classified in terms of home value were 73.5 upper, 64.5 upper–middle, 69.3 middle, 60.5 lower–middle, and 59.7 lower —figures quite similar to Nixon's 1960 percentages: 76.3 upper, 65.4 upper–middle, 70.5 middle, 62.0 lower–middle, and 58.2 lower.[14]

Clearly, Martin ran very close to Nixon, sustaining losses of less than 3 percentage–points at the upper–income interval, and losses of less than

2 percentage–points at the next three income intervals. Martin actually did better than Nixon
among lower–status whites. Though slight, his
gain at the lower–status interval is evidence of the
importance of the racial prodrome in this election,
since the voters lodged in this stratum, in contrast
to upper–status whites, have little liking for con-
servative economic doctrines, and yet they are the
ones who are the most immediately and directly
affected by the implementation of civil rights
policies and are likely, therefore, to regard race
as an issue of utmost importance. This is not to
say, of course, that racial hostility does not influence the political perceptions of higher–status
whites. Quite obviously it does.[15] But strong racial
anxiety is very probably more widespread and of
a higher intensity at the bottom than at the top of
the status scale. Thus, when race is a significant
factor, lower–status white voters may be expected
to divide politically in much the same way as
higher–status whites, but probably for different
reasons. Furthermore, the outcomes of elections in
which race has differential significance almost
certainly differ according to the magnitude of
status polarization.[16] One would expect status
polarization to decline in contests in which race is
of high import, and to increase when race excites
relatively little interest.

The soundness of this assumption can be tested

to some extent with data drawn from Birmingham and other cities of the Deep South. Taking as a very rough measure of status polarization the percentage–point spread in the Republican vote from the upper– to lower–status intervals, one comes away with the finding that in Birmingham the relationship between class and the vote declined in amplitude from Nixon to Martin.[17] The distance from Nixon's support at the upper– and lower–status levels amounted to 18.1 percentage–points. In Martin's case, the figure was 13.8 percentage–points. Thus, there was a decline of 4.3 percentage–points from 1960 to 1962. This differential was not of spectacular proportions, but it was a preview of one aspect of the Goldwater outcome in cities of the Deep South.

In Birmingham, the Goldwater candidacy virtually eliminated polarization of the vote along status lines. In its place there appeared what may be termed, given the direction of the Negro vote, polarization by race. Goldwater drew his heaviest support from among lower–income white voters, but he received overwhelming proportions of the vote in all status categories. His percentages were clustered around the 80 per cent level as follows: 82 upper, 79.5 upper–middle, 83.6 middle, 80.5 lower–middle, and 85.7 lower. The distance from the upper to the lower intervals totaled a minus 3.7 percentage–points, for a decline in status polarization relative to Nixon of 21.8—a figure indicative of the impact of the racial prodrome upon this Deep South metropolitan electorate, and particularly upon its lower–status component. Seemingly, racial hostility had driven all other considerations from the minds of many lower–status whites, causing them to rally to the Goldwater standard with greater over–all enthusiasm than voters did at the other end of the income scale. Considering the high level of support of Nixon and Eisenhower by more prosperous urbanites, it seems likely that many of them would have supported Goldwater had there been no race issue at all; but it is not possible to determine exactly, on the basis of survey data available as this is written, the relative impact of racial and economic issues on the political perceptions and decisions of upper–status metropolitan voters.

Of the Deep South cities considered in this analysis, Jackson, Mississippi, Shreveport, Louisiana, and Mobile, Alabama, rank with Birmingham as cities in which the race issue was most obviously of major concern to white voters in 1964.

In Jackson, Goldwater received almost all of the white vote regardless of status differentiations. Indeed, his proportions of the white vote were truly phenomenal: all but the lower–status vote lodged in the 90 percentile, his best being the 93.4

TABLE 7: Goldwater and Nixon in Deep South Cities *

City	Year	Upper %R	N	Upper–Middle %R	N	Middle %R	N	Lower–Middle %R	N	Lower %R	N	Changes In Status Polarization 1960–1964
Birmingham	1960	76.3	3	65.4	1	70.5	3	62.0	11	58.2	5	−21.8
	1964	81.98		79.5		83.6		80.5		85.7		
Charleston	1960	84.8	2	65.9	2	73.3	1	66.2	1	63.4	1	−7.5
	1964	88.7		78.4		80.9		73.3		74.8		
Columbia	1960	——	0	80.8	2	74.8	2	72.9	5	65.7	3	−3.6
	1964	——		80.1		72.5		74.2		68.6		
Gadsden	1960	——	0	61.8	1	50.6	3	38.3	2	25.1	10	−13.9
	1964	——		77.7		71.9		66.5		54.9		
Jackson	1960	60.9	3	55.0	4	54.1	5	37.8	14	35.4	2	−16.3
	1964	90.7		91.6		91.5		93.4		81.5		
Mobile	1960	——	0	64.9	1	59.8	3	43.7	3	40.2	2	−20.7
	1964	——		81.3		76.97		75.6		77.3		
Montgomery	1960	——	0	——	0	60.7	1	60.5	4	41.0	1	−4.9
	1964	——		——		90.6		85.02		75.8		
Shreveport	1960	78.5	2	74.7	6	69.1	6	47.7	10	46.4	3	−29.6
	1964	88.4		86.4		86.4		86.8		85.9		

* Metropolitan presidential election returns were obtained from newspapers.

per cent that he rolled–up in the lower–middle interval. Nixon, by contrast, received only 37.8 per cent of this vote, and only 35.4 per cent at the lower–status interval. An additional indication of racial polarization was the 16.3 percentage–point decline in status polarization from 1960.

Polarization by race was also the most conspicuous feature of the Goldwater vote in Shreveport, Louisiana, where all of Goldwater's percentages were grouped in the 80 percentile. Goldwater, like Nixon, did best in upper–status Shreveport; but in 1960, 32.1 percentage–points separated the upper– and lower–status invervals, whereas in 1964 the distance was only 2.5 percentage–points. This means that Shreveport experienced a larger decline in status polarization from 1960 to 1964 than any other Deep South city (29.6 percentage–points).

In Mobile, Alabama, as well, status polarization declined sharply from 1960 to 1964, during which period the spread between presidential Republicanism at the upper– and lower–status intervals narrowed from 24.7 percentage–points to a mere 4.0.

In Charleston and Columbia, South Carolina, and in Gadsden and Montgomery, Alabama, the other Deep South cities whose voting behavior was examined, the differences between 1960 and

1964 were somewhat less extreme. Indeed, in these cities the data reveal elements of continuity as well as change. There was evidence of continuity in the fact that Goldwater received his most substantial support from higher–status white voters. Moreover, the differential between the upper– and lower–status intervals were relatively large, exceeding 10 percentage–points in each of the cities. But change was also revealed by the data, much of it attributable to racial concerns. A decline of status polarization in 1964 compared to 1960 is one indication that race was a factor. In percentage–point terms, the decline was heaviest in Gadsden, least marked in Columbia. Apart from having the smallest drop–off in status polarization, Columbia's voting patterns were unique in another respect, for this was the only city in which Goldwater dropped below Nixon among upper–middle and middle–status white voters and was only marginally stronger at the two lower intervals. Even discounting for compensatory shifts, it would still appear that Nixon achieved maximum penetration in this city's electorate in 1960. In cities other than Columbia, Goldwater improved upon Nixon at all status intervals. Invariably, however, his largest gains were in the lower–status wards and precincts; all of these gains were of sufficient magnitude to lift this vote

above majority proportions—additional evidence
of the major formative influence of feelings about
the race issue on the 1964 outcome.[18]

In sum, the data of Table 7, together with data
presented earlier, provide support for the proposition that the Goldwater outcome in the Deep South
more nearly fits the traditional mold of southern
political behavior than it fits the alignments of the
1952–1960 period. A politics of section, whether
based on race or some other shared interest, tends
to bring together men of all social strata in a
single political party. Sectional cohesiveness pro-
duces multi–class electoral outcomes. It is in this
respect that the Goldwater outcome resembles
traditional voting patterns. In 1964, the Deep–
South vote polarized around race. The Goldwater
candidacy alienated Negroes, while simulta-
neously bringing together the white voters from all
status levels who had been angered by the racial
policies of Presidents Kennedy and Johnson.

Antagonism toward the national Democratic
Party was of such a high intensity in the Deep
South that a number of Democratic candidates at
the grassroots level were hurt by it. Seven of the
ten new seats won by the Republican congressional party were added by Deep South electorates,
and in addition, impressive numbers of local Republicans were elected.

However, even as most white voters in the Deep

South were in open revolt against the party of
most of their forebears, voters in the six non–Deep
South states were returning majorities for the
Democratic presidential ticket. Three of these
states—i.e., Florida, Tennessee, and Virginia—
went Democratic for the first time since 1948. In
rejecting Goldwater for Johnson, and thereby
frustrating the Republicans' southern strategy,
several non–Deep South electorates produced voting patterns resembling those of the Eisenhower–
Nixon years.

CHAPTER III

Voting Patterns in the "non–Deep" South

THERE ARE SEVERAL INDICATIONS IN our data of a "milder" outcome in the non–Deep South—that is, there was less evidence of change in voting alignments, more evidence of continuity.

In the first place, the heavy shifts to Goldwater that were revealed by election returns from the Deep South (Table 1) did not occur in the non–

Deep South (Table 8). Instead of a surge of
Republican votes in the latter subregion, there
was a general decline from 1960 except in the
black–belt, and even in this sector the Republican gain was only 10.6 percentage–points, an increase that was not large enough to raise the
Republican proportion of the black–belt vote to
the fortieth percentile. Comparing the Goldwater
vote in the two black–belts, we find that he ran
roughly 34 percentage–points better in the Deep
South.

An equally striking feature of the Goldwater
outcome in the non–Deep South was that he obtained higher levels of support in traditionally–
Republican domain and the metropolitan and
non–metropolitan sectors than in the black–belt
—this despite the fact that his percentages outside the black–belt fell below the levels attained
by Nixon. The Republican drop–offs from 1960
outside the black–belt were of about equivalent
size, amounting to just under 10 percentage–
points in each sector, a difference of less than 1
per cent between the largest loss and the smallest.
These declines had the effect of depressing Goldwater's percentages in all sectors of the non–Deep
South below his percentages in comparable sectors of the Deep South. By way of contrast, both
Nixon and Eisenhower had elicited higher degrees

of enthusiasm from non–Deep South electorates than from voters in the Deep South.

The last, and probably most persuasive, indication of a milder outcome in the non–Deep South was the arrangement of Goldwater's percentages, which, when ranked in descending order by sector, followed in the same sequence as those of Nixon and of Eisenhower. With specific reference to this array, the Goldwater outcome did not upset pre–1964 alignments in the non–Deep South.

These evidences of continuity in the 1964 outcome in the non–Deep South are confirmed in some measure by voting patterns in North Carolina, Tennessee, and Texas. As reported in Table 9, within North Carolina and Texas the Goldwater vote divided in about the same way as at the subregional level. In fact, this had been the shape of the vote in these two states from the time of Alf

TABLE 8: Presidential Republicanism in the Non–Deep South—1952–1964

Sector	Gold-water	Nixon	Eisenhower 1956	1952	%–Point Gain, or Loss 1960–1964
Traditional	49.9	59.2	61.02	58.7	−9.3
Metropolitan	42.3	50.7	57.1	55.04	−8.4
Non–Metropolitan	41.4	49.99	46.96	46.03	−8.5
Black–Belt	37.9	27.3	29.4	29.6	+10.6

Landon's presidential candidacy. This also had
been the pattern in Tennessee since Thomas E.
Dewey's first race in 1944, except that Goldwater
did better in this state's two black–belt counties
than in its non–metropolitan sector—as Eisenhower and Nixon had done in 1952.

Further, though Goldwater fared much less well
than Nixon did throughout Texas, and suffered
moderate–to–heavy losses in non–black–belt Tennessee and in traditionally–Republican and metropolitan North Carolina, Republican declines in
these states were less disruptive of pre–1964 voter
alignments than were the drop–offs in Arkansas,
Florida, and Virginia. Republicans from Willkie
to Nixon in Arkansas, and from Dewey (1948)
to Nixon in Virginia, had elicited support from
each sector that when set in order of size corre-
sponded to the subregional norm. However, this
was not the pattern in 1964.

In Virginia, Goldwater lost heavily to Nixon
in the cities (11.9 percentage–points) and in traditionally–Republican domain (9.8 percentage–
points); experienced a moderate decline (3.5 percentage–points) in the non–metropolitan sector;
and gained (9.9 percentage–points) in the black–
belt. As a result of these shifts to–and–from the
Republicans, Goldwater's percentages in Virginia
dropped–off from the non–metropolitan area to
the traditional counties to the black–belt and

TABLE 9: Goldwater in the non–Deep South States

Sector	State					
	Ark.	Fla.	N. C.	Tenn.	Texas	Va.
Traditional	48.1	—	48.97	52.4	38.8 (41.2)*	47.2
Metropolitan	50.02	46.3	43.3	43.3	38.7 (40.6)*	40.8
Non–Metropolitan	41.5	53.4	41.1	31.4	33.2 (38.9)*	48.4
Black–Belt	44.2	53.2	26.9	51.0	30.1	45.4

* Republican percentage when Roman Catholic counties omitted.

TABLE 10: Goldwater and Nixon in the non–Deep South States: Republican %–Point Gain or Loss in Sectors of the Six non–Deep South States, 1960–1964

Sector	%–Point Gain or Loss 1960–1964					
	Ark.	Fla.	N. C.	Tenn.	Texas	Va.
Traditional	−16.5	—	−7.9	−10.0	−19.7	−9.8
Metropolitan	+5.7	−4.9	−6.9	−4.9	−12.4	−11.9
Non–Metropolitan	−1.3	+1.2	+0.4	−8.1	−10.5	−3.5
Black–Belt	+16.1	+10.3	+7.8	+10.3	−11.6	+9.9

cities.[1] In Arkansas, the black–belt electorate produced the largest Republican gain from 1960 (16.1 percentage–points) of any sector in the subregion; whereas its traditional electorate responded to Goldwater at a level 16.5 percentage–points below Nixon—a loss second only to that of traditional Texas in magnitude.

Non–metropolitan Arkansas, and comparable

sectors of North Carolina and Florida, divided
for Goldwater in about the same proportion as
for Nixon. In the first two states the non–metropolitan Republican vote in 1964 was of about
identical proportions, 41 per cent.

In non–metropolitan Florida, on the other
hand, Goldwater, Nixon and Eisenhower before
him, won majorities. In 1960, non–metropolitan
presidential Republicanism in Florida pulled
ahead of the metropolitan variety for the first time
since 1932, but the differential in 1960 was only
1 percentage–point; in 1964, however, a slight
non–metropolitan shift to Goldwater, coupled
with a moderate decline in the cities, sharpened
the differential between urban and non–urban
Florida to 7 percentage–points. The Republican
decline in metropolitan Florida, together with the
heavy shift to Goldwater in the black–belt of that
state, had the further effect of dropping metropolitan presidential Republicanism below the
black–belt variety for the first time in the twentieth
century.

The indications of continuity as well as change
contained in the statewide data presented in
Tables 9 and 10 were for the most part corrobo-
rated by correlations of the Republican presidential vote from 1956 to 1960 and from 1960 to
1964 in each of the non–Deep South states.

	R, 1956–60	R, 1960–64
Arkansas	.74	.05
Florida	.91	.03
North Carolina	.96	.86
Tennessee	.94	.91
Texas	.66 (.72)	.74 (.77)
Virginia	.82	.41

In North Carolina and Tennessee, correlation, of Eisenhower and Nixon (elections of 1956 and 1960) and Nixon and Goldwater (elections of 1960 and 1964) yielded coefficients suggestive of a high degree of stability in the presidential Republicanism of counties within these states in the 1956, 1960, and 1964 presidential elections. In Texas, while the coefficient linking Eisenhower to Nixon was suggestive of a relationship, it was of significantly lesser magnitude than those in other states, and it was not of the magnitude of the coefficient that related Nixon to Goldwater. This may be explained in part—but only in part—by the shifting preferences of Roman Catholic voters in the state. That is, Roman Catholics in Texas, as in Louisiana, generally favored Eisenhower in 1956, switched to Kennedy in 1960, and remained with the Democratic presidential party and Lyndon Johnson in 1964. Thus, when counties having Catholic populations of 40 per cent or more are removed from the data of Table 12,

Goldwater's proportion of the vote increases in sectors in which these counties are situated. Similarly, correlations of 1956–1960 and 1960–1964 without the Catholic counties raises the coefficients in amplitude. The increments are of small degree, however, indicating that in Texas, as in Louisiana, factors other than religion account for much of the variance in the vote from 1956 through 1964.

Elsewhere in the non–Deep South, Nixon had related to Eisenhower at significant levels in Arkansas, Florida, and Virginia. Yet, there was little correlation between Nixon and Goldwater in the first two states, and only a tenuous connection in Virginia. That is, in Arkansas, Florida, and Virginia the Goldwater candidacy had the effect of disrupting pre–1964 voting alignments. But, considering the total picture, in these states (as throughout the non–Deep South) the 1964 outcomes represented less drastic repudiations of the past than those which took place in the Deep South.

Comparison of the aggregate election results in the Deep South and in the non–Deep South indicates that by and large the electorates of the two subregions differed in their perceptions of the candidates, the issues, or both. In the Deep South particularly, indications are that for the mass of voters the race question was considered of major importance, and that many voters made their choice solely on the basis of this issue. Race was also an important consideration in the non–Deep South and, as we have seen, left its imprint upon the election returns—and yet much less decisively than in the Deep South.

Philip E. Converse, Aage Clausen, and Warren Miller considered the race issue in the South in their "Electoral Myth and Reality: The 1964 Election", using as their source of data the southern component of the Survey Research Center's 1964 sample of the national electorate. They found that:

> . . . civil rights, while the primary issue in the South, was not the only one. Beyond civil rights, southerners reacted negatively to the Goldwater positions much as their fellow citizens elsewhere. Many southern white respondents said in effect: 'Goldwater is right on the black man, and that is very important. But he is so wrong on everything else I can't bring myself to vote for him.' [2]

While Converse, Clausen, and Miller did not locate voters holding this viewpoint within the region, the aggregate returns examined thus far strongly suggest that most of them probably resided in states of the non–Deep South. Additional support for this speculation is to be found in the

election returns drawn from the subregion's counties grouped by non–white registration (Tables 11
and 12), and from its cities (Table 13).

With reference to presidential Republicanism
and non–white registration, Table 11 displays the
Goldwater and Nixon vote as well as the Republican shifts from 1960 to 1964 at intervals of non–
white registration in counties of Arkansas, Florida,
and Virginia (the only states for which registration
data by race are available). A similar treatment of
the Republican vote in the black–belt counties of
these states appears in Table 12.

There are several indications in Table 11 that
the racial question carried less weight with voters
in the non–Deep South. One of them is the absence
of a precise relationship between the Goldwater
vote and Negro registration. Another is the moderate spread of only 8 percentage–points between
Goldwater's vote at the extremes of the classification. Still another indication is the direct relationship of the Republican shifts 1960–to–1964
to the classification. All of these features of the
data represent striking departures from the Deep
South results as shown in Table 5. In the Deep
South the Goldwater vote was related inversely to
non–white registration, and the distance from
his vote at the extremes of the classification
amounted to fully 26 percentage–points. We have
interpreted these characteristics of the Goldwater

TABLE 11: Republican Proportions of the Total Presidential Vote in Counties of Three non–Deep South States Classified by Percentage Negro of Total Registration

Negro % Total Registration	Number of Counties	Per Cent Republican 1964	1960	%–Point Gain 1960–1964
40 or more	5	38.1	29.7	8.4
30–39	15	43.2	35.9	7.2
20–29	45	47.3	43.7	3.7
10–19	92	49.5	47.6	1.9
0–9	114	46.2	54.3	−8.1

TABLE 12: Republican Proportion of the Total Presidential Vote in Black–Belt Counties of Three non–Deep South States Classified by Percentage Negro of Total Registration

Negro % Total Registration	Number of Counties	Per Cent Republican 1964	1960	%–Point Gain 1960–1964
40 or more	5	38.1	29.7	8.42
30–39	8	43.2	35.4	7.8
20–29	6	52.6	42.7	9.7
10–19	3	52.7	41.6	11.1

Data source for non–white registration: *United States Commission on Civil Rights,* Information Center, Washington, D.C., March 19, 1965. The registration figures for counties of Arkansas and Virginia are estimates.

outcome to mean that the subregion's electorate polarized around the race issue, with almost all Negroes voting Democratic and the overwhelming majority of whites going for Goldwater. Republican shifts from 1960 to 1964 fit the broad contours of this interpretation very well. Thus, the Goldwater gain was as much as 27 percentage–points in counties with few Negro registrants, and only 11 percentage–points in counties where Negro registration was heavy.

In the non–Deep South, however, this pattern was reversed, with Goldwater gaining up to 8 percentage–points at the high intervals of non–white registration and losing a like number of percentage–points at the low interval of non–white registration. By following the reasoning underlying our interpretation of the Deep South results, one might conclude that Goldwater was picking up Negro votes in the non–Deep South, but this explanation may be summarily dismissed; as indicated below, Negro voters in the non–Deep South were as lacking in enthusiasm for Goldwater as their counterparts in the Deep South.

The pattern of Republican shifts in the non–Deep South becomes intelligible if one considers the possibility that race was *not* the sole determinant of the vote division among white electorates, particularly those residing outside the black–belt. If race was in fact not the only polarizing issue, then it would appear that many white voters living in counties having few Negro registrants rejected Goldwater for reasons having little or nothing to do with race. Contrariwise,

Goldwater had a greater appeal for white electorates living in counties with heavy Negro concentration where race was a more significant component of the electoral decisions of white voters, and where Goldwater improved upon Nixon's showing. It follows from this interpretation of the data that non–Deep South black–belt voting behavior should resemble the Deep South variety. Thus, in Table 12 the Republican shifts and vote relate inversely to non–white registration in the black–belt. Here again, however, the results indicate that even within the black–belt electorate of the non–Deep South the racial question was less decisive than it was for white voters in the Deep South.

Goldwater received only bare majorities of the vote in black–belt counties having the smallest proportion of Negro registrants, whereas he won upwards of two–thirds of the vote in comparable black–belt counties of the Deep South. Furthermore, the statistical distance between the extremes of the non–Deep South, black–belt classification was appreciably shorter than it had been in the Deep South—14.6 percentage–points in the former, 52.8 percentage–points in the latter. At least some non–Deep South black–belt whites apparently behaved in the manner described by the Survey Research Center; that is, they voted for Johnson despite whatever racial anxieties they

TABLE 13: Goldwater and Nixon in non-Deep South Cities [a]

City	Year	Income Level										Changes In Status Polarization 1960–1964
		Upper %R	N	Upper–Middle %R	N	Middle %R	N	Lower–Middle %R	N	Lower %R	N	
Asheville	1960	——	0	64.5	1	57.9	1	56.6	4	53.5	4	−0.9
	1964			43.99		43.9		39.6		33.9		
Charlotte	1960	78.9	4	77.6	1	64.01	5	57.95	11	46.3	9	−15.4
	1964	64.3		66.1		56.4		53.8		47.1		
Chattanooga	1962 [b]	——	0	——	0	63.1	3	57.6	4	48.3	12	−14.3
	1964					54.3		59.1		53.8		
Dallas	1960	77.2	1	78.1	5	74.1	8	64.3	16	54.9	10	+5.4
	1964	61.0		61.1		57.6		47.3		33.3		
Memphis	1960	75.7	3	69.4	5	67.7	9	58.7	29	57.9	24	−16.2
	1964	72.2		70.5		60.9		65.7		70.6		
Roanoke	1960	79.9	1	75.1	2	75.4	3	66.9	10	54.6	12	−0.5
	1964	71.1		73.3		61.8		53.96		46.3		

[a] Metro presidential election returns were obtained from newspapers.
[b] Republican Congressional vote, 1962.

might have had. All of this must, of course, be hedged in with appropriate cautions, for we have been dealing with white and Negro behavior in only half of the six non–Deep South states, and the registration data for two of them are estimates rather than official tabulations.

The direction of the Negro vote in the non–Deep South is considerably less problematical. It was solidly Democratic. Goldwater received only 1.7 per cent of the total vote cast in twenty–four Negro "Tag" precincts in cities of five non–Deep South states. Measuring from 1960 to 1964, the drop–off in Negro presidential Republicanism amounted to 20.6 percentage–points—a figure of substantial size, and yet well below the loss of 51.8 percentage–points in the Deep South. Considering this very substantial difference in the magnitude of Republican drop–offs among Negro voters of the two subregions, one may readily infer the need to modify the conclusion derived from the 1960 outcome regarding the shift of Negroes from Eisenhower to Kennedy. The 1960 exodus of Negro voters from the Republican presidential party now appears to have been more pronounced as a feature of Negro voting in the non–Deep South than it was in the entire region.[3]

In 1964, every election forecaster predicted that the voting behavior of Negroes in general, and of urban Negroes in particular, would not be favor-

able to the Republicans. The election returns
justified the predictions, as Negro presidential Republicanism declined to new lows in both subregions of the South. Similarly, in cities of the
Deep South, the conspicuous feature of the data
was its unidirectional quality, with the white vote
moving toward Goldwater at all status intervals.
Though Deep South whites failed to support Goldwater at levels as high as those at which Negroes
supported Johnson, the white urban vote was, by
any interpretation, overwhelmingly Republican,
especially in Birmingham, Jackson, and Shreveport. In these cities, so–called "block voting" was
almost as prevalent among whites as it was among
Negroes. As a result of the high degree of racial
polarization of Deep South metropolitan electorates, status polarization declined from the levels
of 1960 in all eight cities where voting behavior
was studied.

In six non–Deep South cities the outcome was
mixed, with white urbanites dividing in ways both
similar and dissimilar to the division of urban
voters in the Deep South.

With regard to the similarities, Table 13 reveals
that in Memphis and Chattanooga the pattern of
the vote resembled typical Deep South voter alignment. That is, presidential Republicanism in the
two Tennessee cities did not break along status
lines. Goldwater had majorities of equivalent pro-

portions at the highest and lowest status intervals in both cities. Since status had related to the vote in Memphis in 1960 and in Chattanooga in 1962, status polarization measured from these earlier years declined by 16.2 percentage–points in Memphis and by 14.3 percentage–points in Chattanooga. This suggests that the race issue had an impact on the election returns, particularly in Memphis. Goldwater ran behind Johnson in Memphis as a whole, but in parts of the city he won majorities of 60 per cent or more, and in lower–status wards he received as many as seven out of ten votes cast. Nixon, in 1960, carried decisively the white electorates of Memphis, but Goldwater did not do as well in the upper– and middle–status wards, and won only about the same proportion of the votes cast in the upper–middle status wards. Significantly from the standpoint of the race issue, it was in the lower–status wards that Goldwater far outdistanced his predecessor.

While Goldwater won a majority in Chattanooga, he was less popular there than in Memphis among white middle–, lower–middle, and lower–status voters, winning a peak percentage of 59 of the lower–middle status vote and only 53 per cent of the vote in lower–status wards. When the presidential vote in Chattanooga is related to the congressional vote division of 1962—an adjustment made necessary by changes in ward bound-

aries in this city—the data show that Goldwater
ran ahead of Republican Congressman Brock's
1962 showing at the lower–status intervals but did
not do so at the middle–status interval. Here again
the most plausible interpretation of the data is
that racial fears were driving lower–status whites
to Goldwater.

In Charlotte, North Carolina, data for 1964 reveal a decline in status polarization, from 1960,
by a heavy 15.4 percentage–points. However, the
pattern of the Goldwater vote in this city differed
significantly in several ways from the voting patterns of Memphis and Chattanooga. In Charlotte,
the Goldwater vote generally related to status divisions, Goldwater ran behind Nixon at all status
intervals, and finally, Goldwater failed to capture
a majority of the lower–status vote—though he
did come close to doing so, as Nixon had in 1960.

When the Goldwater vote is compared to that
for Nixon in the three remaining cities, it appears
that status polarization either increased (Dallas),
or remained at about the level of 1960 (Asheville and Roanoke). Though there were only
light–to–moderate changes in status polarization
in these cities, the white urban vote in each displayed considerable variance, all of which can be
attributed to declines in presidential Republicanism from 1960. The Republican losses were of
substantial size, exceeding 10 percentage–points

at the various status intervals of each city except in upper–middle and upper–status Roanoke, where the losses totaled 1.8 and 8.8 percentage–points respectively. The fact that the Republican vote in Asheville, Dallas, and Roanoke declined rather than increased from 1960 means that the Goldwater percentages at the various status intervals in these three cities were all of lesser magnitude than in cities of the Deep South. The contrast between the two subregions' cities was usually sharpest at the lower–status intervals but a differential response to Goldwater was also detectable in the voting behavior of upper–status whites. This is particularly evident in the figures for Goldwater's upper–status support in Asheville and Dallas, as contrasted with his support among comparable electorates in the Deep South.

In sum, declines in metropolitan presidential Republicanism from 1960 to 1964 lend support to the proposition that a large segment of the non–Deep South white electorate had a broad range of concerns including, but not limited to, the issues having to do with race. For many voters, it is likely that factors other than race were decisive in determining the direction of their vote.

But to say that many white voters in the non–Deep South had a multiplicity of worries, of which race was only one, is not to deny that the race issue was of considerable importance to the white

electorate of the subregion. A report issued by the
Southern Regional Council, entitled "What Happened in the South?", asserts that:

> Arkansas, Florida, Tennessee, and Virginia clearly would have gone Republican had it not been
> for the Negro vote. One other, North Carolina,
> might have. Only in President Johnson's home
> state of Texas among the eleven states of the
> South did the Democratic Party clearly receive
> the majority of white votes.[4]

Evidence of the impact of the issue of race is
sprinkled throughout the returns from the subregion's black–belt and from its cities. Indeed the
amount of the Republican shift from 1960 to
1964 as observed in our data and attributed to
race is probably much less than 100 per cent of
the change accounted for by this one issue.

Distortion in our statistical impression of the
impact of race upon the vote is the result of at
least two changing components of the southern
electoral situation. One of them is the expansion
of the electorate since 1960, the other is shifting
voter preferences from 1960 to 1964. The proportion of observable change would have been depressed if either or both of these elements had
compensatory effects. It is likely that this was the
case, particularly in the black–belt of the non–
Deep South. Attention to the Republican vote in

this sector over time will reveal a lesser amount of change than in any other sector of the two sub-regions 2.3 per cent from 1952 to 1960. In part, the stability of this vote and the relatively small GOP gain over the period from 1960 to 1964 may be explained by a heavy Negro registration. A substantial Negro vote would, in turn, introduce the possibility of compensatory voting by whites that to some extent may have submerged white black–belt support for Goldwater under a wave of Negro votes for President Johnson.

It is likely that similar distortions are woven into the voting patterns of other sectors of the two subregions. There is a reason to suppose, how-ever, that distortion resulting from compensatory shifts was less marked in the Deep South, where levels of Negro registration were generally lower. It may be presumed that if the Negro vote were completely removed from our data, then Gold-water's showing might well compare more favor-ably to Nixon's in both subregions—but especially in the non–Deep South.

But how much more favorably? This question may have been answered by the Southern Re-gional Council [4] for the four states of Arkansas, Florida, Tennessee, and Virginia. *If* the Negro registration in these four states did exceed Demo-cratic pluralities, and *if* all or almost all Ne-gro registrants voted, then the Negro was, without doubt, the decisive factor in Goldwater's loss of four non–Deep South states. From another standpoint, however, Goldwater could perhaps have carried Arkansas, Florida, Tennessee, Virginia, and other non–Deep South states, despite the Negro vote, *if* white electorates had shifted as monolithically toward the Republican Party as white voters did in the Deep South.

But non–Deep southerners did not rally to Goldwater with anything like the enthusiasm of their neighbors in the Deep South. This is the most prominent feature of the election returns from the non–Deep South. Neither its black–belt, nor metropolitan, nor non–metropolitan nor traditionally–Republican electorates supplied Goldwater with percentages of their vote comparable in size to those which he elicited from the counterparts of these electorates in the Deep South. Goldwater won majorities in only five of the subregion's twenty–three sectors, and did less well than Nixon had in fifteen of them. Particularly damaging to his chances in states where he had majorities were his failures to carry sectors that contribute decisive or critical proportions of the actual electorate. In the one instance where he carried a critical sector, his majority was not large enough to offset Democratic pluralities elsewhere in the state. Thus, in Arkansas Goldwater had a thin majority (50.02 per cent) of the metropolitan vote,

but only 41 per cent in the non–metropolitan
sector. Differential support for his candidacy on
the part of urbanites and non–urbanites was of
crucial significance, inasmuch as non–metropolitan Arkansas contributes about three–fourths of
the state's actual electorate, and the metropolitan
contribution is less than one–fifth (18.3 per cent).

A divergent set of relationships prevailed in
Florida, in terms of Goldwater's vote and in terms
of the structure of the state's actual electorate.
Goldwater won a majority of 53.4 per cent of the
non–metropolitan vote, 46 per cent in the cities.
Unfortunately for the implementation of Goldwater's southern strategy, however, Florida's cities
provide the decisive component of its actual electorate, just under two–thirds (63.7 per cent),
while its non–metropolitan counties contribute
just over one–third (35.7 per cent).

In Tennessee, Goldwater carried the traditionally–Republican sector, which in this state sup-
plies more than two–fifths (44.8 per cent) of the
total vote—a proportion larger than that contributed by any other sector. But his majority in this
sector, 52.4 per cent, was the lowest achieved by
any Republican presidential nominee since Wen-
dell Willkie, and was well below the level he
needed to compensate for his deficits in the cities,
where he received only 43.3 per cent of the vote,
and in the countryside where his share amounted

to only 31.4 per cent—two sectors that combined
have a majority (54.3 per cent) of the state's actual electorate. Goldwater's black–belt majority
in Tennessee was of very little importance, since
this sector contains only two counties whose voters constitute less than 1 per cent of the state's
total electorate.

The structure of the actual electorate is important in non–Deep South states other than Arkansas, Florida, and Tennessee only if one imputes
majorities to Goldwater by removing the Negro
vote from the election returns. Giving this treatment to the data would almost certainly elevate
Republican percentages of the vote to majority
proportions in the metropolitan, non–metropolitan, and black–belt sectors of several states. It
would, however, have little effect upon his showing in the traditionally–Republican counties, since
few Negroes live in the party's mountain strong-
holds, and those who do constitute a small proportion of the registered electorate. Historically,
race has not been the burning issue in these areas
as it has been in the lowlands. As V. O. Key
put it:

> The yeoman of the hills was reluctant to aban-
> don the Union for the cause of the planter and
> his slaves. When the people voted on secession
> or related issues, the upland farmers showed
> hostility toward secession or at least far less en-

thusiasm than the lowlands. . . . The highland yeo-
manry did not want to fight a rich man's war;
the Democratic Party was, or at least became,
the planter's party and the war party. The Democratic Party forced the hills into The War and for
this it has never been forgiven. There is, of
course, more than the recollection of war underlying the Republicanism of the hills.[5]

Key identified traditionally–Republican terrain
with a radical tradition having "little in common
with the manufacturing–financial orientation of
the party nationally" [6]—and, one might add, little
in common with the tradition of hostility toward
the Negro in the Deep South.

Thus, neither Goldwater's extreme economic
conservatism nor his "states' rights" attitudes had
much appeal for the "yeomen of the hills", and it is
not surprising that in four non–Deep South states
Goldwater sustained his heaviest losses from
Nixon in traditionally–Republican territory. In
the fifth state having traditionally–Republican
counties, Virginia, the Republican drop–off from
1960 in those counties was 9.8 percentage–points
—a decline second only to that of 11.9 percentage–points sustained in the cities. Indeed, considering the origins of traditional–Republicanism in
the South, it is in some ways surprising that Goldwater did as well as he did in these counties. His
majority in Tennessee and his near misses in

Arkansas, North Carolina, and Virginia stand out as noteworthy illustrations of the power of party labels as such, and of the persistence of political affiliations acquired by inheritance, entirely apart from the merits of either the candidates or the issues in particular elections.

CHAPTER IV

Convergence and Divergence

THE GOLDWATER OUTCOME CON-
tained a mixture of continuity and change. The
1964 presidential election brought out in bold
relief differential political responses from the Old
and the New South. For decades urbanization and
industrialization, migration, and the mechaniza-
tion and diversification of agriculture have been
among the forces changing the socio–economic

face of the South, creating the environment for a
more competitive regional politics. But the pace at
which the South has been moving from a rural–
agrarian setting to one that is more urban–industrial has varied considerably from state–to–state.

This differential development of the South is
captured in a general way by dividing the region
into subregions, for on balance Deep South states
have lagged behind non–Deep South states in
their socio–economic development. Most importantly, it is the five Deep South states which
continue to hold a majority (51.2 in 1960) of
the region's Negro population, each state having
non–white concentrations greater than 30 per
cent of their total population. This Negro concentration and the complex of white attitudes as-
sociated with the Negro and his place in southern
society gave Deep South voting patterns their distinctive regional coloration in 1964. The salience
of race for the mass public of the Deep South was
made abundantly clear by the election returns.
Race was a force strong enough to override whatever misgivings many white Deep South voters
may have had about Senator Goldwater's economic views. In the absence of race, attitudes
toward economic issues might have weighed
heavily against Goldwater as a component of the
electorate's decision, for it has been a finding of
survey research that, apart from race, "the South

takes positions in mass opinion on broad questions of policy remarkably similar to those of the nation".[1]

Equally apparent from the election returns is the fact that race had a lower prominence in mass opinion in the non–Deep South. To a degree higher than in the Deep South, white hostility toward the Negro in the non–Deep South received both cover and concealment from its larger Negro electorate. Even discounting for a monolithic Negro Democratic vote, race was in the aggregate less significant as a component of the electoral decision in the non–Deep South. Lower racial salience in this subregion may be explained partly by the fact that its white electorates generally possess a less distinctive regional outlook than those of the Deep South and vote more nearly alike voters elsewhere in the nation.

In this regard, the year 1964 appears to have been a further step on the road to the "nationalization" of presidential politics in the non–Deep South. As shown in Figure 2a, the modification of political sectionalism has been underway in the non–Deep South at least since 1920 and possibly before that as well. Over the last four decades non–Deep South voting patterns have generally followed the national shifts of Republican fortunes. The parallel has not been exact, nor would this have been a reasonable expectation, given the

long–standing commitment of most southern voters to the Democratic Party. Yet, the data of Figure 2a clearly indicate that voters in the non–Deep
South have come to behave politically more like
non–southerners.

Figure 2: GOP Presidential Vote in Southern Subregions

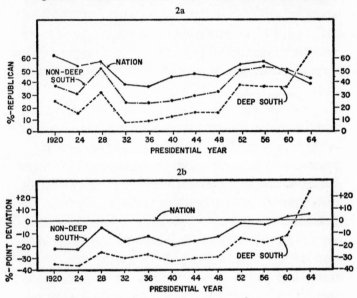

Philip Converse has termed the process
"whereby the South might slip more directly into
the mainstream of American political life" the
convergence outcome.[2] Using the aggregate vote
division since 1920 we have sought to test for convergence in Figure 2a. Another treatment of the

data, one that underscores the movement toward convergence, is shown in Figure 2b; there the Republican vote in the subregions is plotted as a deviation from the national Republican vote. While the movement of the non–Deep South in the direction of the nation is irregular, with cyclical variations reflecting the impact of short–term forces such as religion in 1928 and Dwight D. Eisenhower in the 1950's, the secular trend toward convergence also is revealed. Thus if a straight line which best fits the data were overlaid on non–Deep South presidential Republicanism in Figure 2a, this "trend" line would feature an inclining slope indicative of this electorate's response to long–term forces that have had continuing adherence from certain categories of southern voters.[3] These forces would include the differential economic orientations of the presidential parties. Long–term influences accounted for a large portion of the secular rise of presidential Republicanism apparent in our data. To be sure, certain electorates of the non–Deep South continue to manifest voting patterns with identifiably southern responses to candidates and issues. In 1960, and again in 1964, the non–Deep South was slightly more Republican than the nation. In the first of what might be called divergent outcomes, at least some voters in the subregion responded, as did many non–southerners, to the reappearance of religion as a short–term force. In 1964, on the other hand, the short–term force contributing to divergence was race. If the actual Negro vote could be taken out of the data for 1964, the gap between presidential Republicanism in the subregion and the nation would widen, but not to the degree of matching the distance between the Deep South variety and that of the nation.

Prior to 1964, the Republican vote in the Deep South, too, had moved with the national drift of voter sentiment. Almost always, however, the Republican vote division in the Deep South was less closely related to the surge and decline of presidential Republicanism in the nation than non–Deep South voting. Indeed, until 1964 Deep South Republicanism had remained at levels below those of the non–Deep South and the nation. The markedly sectional reaction of the Deep South to Goldwater, for the first time elevated the subregion's presidential Republicanism to a plateau 23.5 percentage–points above that of the nation. This surge of Republicans, when viewed from the standpoint of the Eisenhower–Nixon outcomes, constituted the major portion of change observed in our data. When placed against the broad sweep of southern history, however, the Deep South's reaction to Goldwater appears as a regression to traditional political behavior with an ironic reversal of roles both for the presidential parties and the subregion's electorates. This time the Republican presidential party wore the mantel of the traditional party of the southern white man, while its Democratic counterpart espoused the cause of the Negro. The subregion's white and Negro electorates responded to these political stimuli in the traditional way.

What of the future? Does the Goldwater outcome enter political history as a cyclical variation, after which southern presidential Republicanism will revert to the level of an earlier period, say the 1940's? Or, did the candidacy of Senator Goldwater bring about a basic alteration in the political preferences of white voters in the Deep South. Is their subregion now more reliably Republican than in the past, while the non–Deep South remains, for the most part, competitive?

One's answers to such questions depend significantly upon the index selected to measure the degree of continuity and change present in the Goldwater outcome. If party identification is the index chosen, then the answer is that the Goldwater candidacy caused a much less than earth–shaking change in the basic division of party loyalties in the region.

In "Electoral Myth and Reality", Converse and associates note that in their data

. . . expressions of party loyalty from the South
which had been slowly losing Democratic strength
throughout the 1950's show a sudden rebound in
1964. However, all of the rebound can be traced
to Southern Negroes; the downward trend among
Southern whites continued and at about the same
pace.[4]

The basis for this interpretation of the impact
of the Goldwater candidacy upon southern electorates is the concept of party identification. Without detracting from the general utility of party
identification as an analytical tool to determine
the underlying division of party loyalties, one may
inquire whether the Deep South component of
national samples was of adequate size to gauge
the total impact of the Goldwater outcome upon
the subregion's white electorates.[5] What, for example, of its white black–belt component? What
of the lower–status white voters in cities like
Birmingham, Alabama, and Jackson, Mississippi,
the vast majority of whom gave their support to
Senator Goldwater and, in the case of Birmingham, to his running mates at the grassroots? Can
the Deep South portion of national surveys tell us
whether their overwhelming endorsement of Goldwater was a short-term defection or a durable
shift in party attachment?

The race issue has, as Converse suggests, "those
characteristics necessary if a political issue is to

form the springboard for large-scale partisan realignment".[6] Heretofore, one basic requirement for
realignment has been missing. Neither major presidential party before 1964 was willing to offer an
alternate that was attractive to racially–oriented
Deep South whites. Even though Senator Goldwater fulfilled this requirement, it is unlikely in
the foreseeable future that a candidate of the
Republican presidential party again will mirror so
closely as did Senator Goldwater the traditional
states' rights views of Deep South white electorates. For this reason, 1964 might well be thought
of as a short-term defection. Lacking a racially
satisfying choice, Deep South whites in the future
may be forced into the two–party mold, or they
may defect to yet another third party. In short,
realignment on anything like a major scale seems
as unlikely after Goldwater as before.[7] Yet, despite the improbability of another presidential candidate so favorable to the Deep South's "states'
rights" viewpoint, several features of the Goldwater outcome and its aftermath suggest a more dynamic impact upon Deep South electorates than
changes in party identification alone imply.

Party identification has remained relatively
stable in the nation since its first reading from
survey data in 1952. Yet the electoral context out
of which party identification is formed has been
dynamic, although not nearly as dynamic nation-

ally as during the Depression period. Donald
Stokes points out that candidates and issues "introduce more dynamism into the contest for the
presidency than the stability of party identification or of the social basis of party preference
might lead us to expect".[8] In the Deep South setting the Goldwater candidacy and the race issue
induced voter shifts from 1960 of greater magnitude than in any other sector of the country. Add
to these shifts the growth of state and local Republican parties and the expansion of the actual
voting population, and it becomes difficult to re-
press skepticism whether survey research has
captured a large portion of the change observed
in Deep South political behavior. This skepticism
holds true even though the party identification of
white southerners was left largely undisturbed by
the Goldwater outcome.

One very dynamic element that the Goldwater
candidacy left behind in the Deep South was a
number of state and local Republican parties de-
monstrably stronger than at any time in the past,
whether measured by votes, contests entered and
won, organization, money, motivation, or even
conversion of Democratic officeholders to Republicanism. As Republican candidates contest for
state and local offices, the party vote and the opportunity for the crystallization of party loyalty
will increase. Already there are indications of

some development of an enduring Republicanism below the presidential level. Republicans have been elected to the state legislatures of Georgia and Mississippi, as mayors in both Columbus and Hattiesburg, Mississippi (both mayoralty candidates were converts from the Democratic Party) and to a scattering of other local offices in this state, and to a congressional seat in South Carolina (the winner also was a convert from Democracy). These are but a handful of Republicans, but the fact that state and local parties are putting forth candidates and winning elections attests to the continued vitality of the Grand Old Party in the subregion. It also testifies emphatically to the determination of Republican managers to construct a strong second party in the Deep South. Republican Party leaders will probably be helped in their efforts to build the party in the Deep South to the extent that racial tensions remain at a high level, and in the short–run the party's ruling elite may be expected to continue the states' rights strategy which proved so successful in 1964. If the unfavorable image of the Democratic Party should rub off on any of its candidates at the grassroots, Democratic officeholders might very well become less numerous in 1966. If, however, racial tensions abate, the developing Republican parties will have to face up to dilemmas of strategy which, while possibly inevitable, have been delayed by the high perception of the race issue by Deep South voters.[9]

In addition to stimulating grassroots Republicanism, the Goldwater candidacy brought out the vote, particularly in the Deep South where the actual electorate increased by almost one–third from 1960 (30.1 per cent). The comparable figure for the non–Deep South was 15.8.[10] While one segment of this increase was accounted for by Negro voters entering the electorate for the first time, another increment consisted of whites, many of whom may well have been peripheral voters attracted by a high stimulus election.[11] Some of these white voters undoubtedly voted as a reaction to heavy Negro registration. As yet, however, we know nothing of the party attachment of these voters, much less of their characteristics or of the possibilities for their continued participation in the politics of the subregion. Nor is it likely that the Deep South component of a national sample can at this time illuminate this segment of the subregion's electorate.

All of this speculation emphasizes that these and other dynamic elements present in the Deep South setting may well have effected changes in party attachment that are not immediately discernible in national survey data. Moreover, in the future these changes will attain visibility only through national surveys having a larger subregional component and through the election returns for 1966 and later years. Of course, the skeptic may take exception to this line of reasoning on the grounds that we have given our data a distinctively subregional interpretation, whereas southern electorates have in fact been responding to political stimuli in much the same way as non–southerners. This was, in fact, the case for many voters in both subregions, and especially in the non–Deep South before 1964. The candidacy of Goldwater and the injection of race into the presidential contest, however, induced the Deep South to move strongly to the Republican side. As a result, what now may well be occurring within the region is the continuing development of non–Deep South Republicanism along urban–industrial lines in which the most enduring party attachments form, as in the past, in the cities and their suburbs. Traditional party ties still persist in the non–metropolitan sectors. The urban development may continue in the Deep South as well, but given the probable short–run strategy of Deep South Republican leadership, there is now the real possibility that an enduring grassroots Republicanism may emerge among the white voters who live in rural areas with heavy Negro concentrations and large Negro electorates. In short, from the 1964 presidential election "pockets of realignment" may emerge within sectors of the Deep

South. The Goldwater outcome and its aftermath are alive with opportunities for analysis and testing of these and other possible directions of southern political behavior.

Notes

INTERDISCIPLINARY BEHAVIORALISM IN
ELECTION RESEARCH

[1] V. O. Key, Jr., *Public Opinion and American Democracy* (New York: Knopf, 1961), p. 458.

[2] Frank J. Sorauf, "American Parties and the Scholar: The Last 30 Years", a paper presented at the annual meeting of the American Political Science Association, September 4–7, 1963, in New York, N.Y.

[3] See Peter Rossi's discussion of "Trends in Voting Behavior Research: 1933–1963", a paper presented at the annual meeting of the American Political Science Association, September 4–7, 1963, in New York, N.Y.

[4] Paul F. Lazarsfeld, Bernard R. Berelson, and Hazel Gaudet, *The People's Choice* (2nd ed.; New York: Columbia University Press, 1948), Bernard R. Berelson, Paul F. Lazarsfeld, and William N. Mc-

Phee, *Voting* (Chicago: University of Chicago Press, 1954); Angus Campbell, Gerald Gurin, and Warren E. Miller, *The Voter Decides* (Evanston, Ill.: Row, Peterson, 1954); Angus Campbell, Philip E. Converse, Warren E. Miller, and Donald E. Stokes, *The American Voter* (New York: Wiley, 1960).

[5] Evron M. Kirkpatrick, "The Impact of the Behavioral Approach on Traditional Political Science", in Austin Ranney, ed., *Essays on the Behavioral Study of Politics* (Urbana: University of Illinois Press, 1962), pp. 10–11.

[6] David Easton, *The Political System* (New York: Knopf, 1953), p. 201.

[7] David B. Truman, Social Science Research Council, *Items* (December, 1951), as quoted in Robert A. Dahl, "The Behavioral Approach in Political Science", *American Political Science Review,* Vol. 55 (December, 1961), p. 767.

[8] Heinz Eulau, *The Behavioral Persuasion in Politics* (New York: Random House, 1963), p. 3.

[9] *Ibid.*, p. 19.

[10] Quoted in Dahl, pp. 767–768.

[11] *Ibid.*, p. 767.

[12] Nelson W. Polsby, Robert A. Dentler, and Paul A. Smith, *Politics and Social Life* (Boston: Houghton Mifflin, 1963), p. 5.

[13] For criticisms of the behavioral approach, see Bernard Crick, *The American Science of Politics, Its Origins and Conditions* (Berkeley: University of California Press, 1959), and Herbert J. Storing, ed., *Essays on the Scientific Study of Politics* (New York: Holt, Rinehart, and Winston, 1962).

[14] Dahl, p. 769.

[15] For an early review and classification of the voting studies see Samuel Eldersveld, "Theory and Method in Voting Behavior Research", *Journal of Politics*, Vol. 13 (February, 1951), pp. 70–87. More recent surveys of voting studies include Seymour M. Lipset, Paul F. Lazarsfeld, Allen H. Barton, and Juan Linz, "The Psychology of Voting: An Analysis of Political Behavior", in Gardner Lindzey, ed., *Handbook of Social Psychology* (Cambridge, Mass.: Addison–Wesley, 1954), Vol. II, pp. 1124–1175; Peter Rossi, "Four Landmarks in Voting Research", in Eugene Burdick and Arthur J. Brodbeck, eds., *American Voting Behavior* (Glencoe: Free Press, 1959); Peter Rossi, "Trends in Voting Behavior Research: 1933–1963"; and Evron Kirkpatrick, "The Impact of the Behavioral Approach on Traditional Political Science".

[16] V. O. Key, Jr., *Southern Politics* (New York: Knopf, 1949); Alexander Heard, *A Two–Party South?* (Chapel Hill: University of North Carolina Press, 1952); Donald S. Strong, *The 1952 Presidential Election in the South* (University, Alabama: Bureau of Public Administration, 1955), and *Urban Republicanism in the South* (University, Alabama: Bureau of Public Administration, 1960).

[17] Frank J. Sorauf, "American Parties and the Scholar: The Last 30 Years", p. 6.

[18] Donald S. Strong, *The 1952 Presidential Election in the South*, p. 382.

[19] *Journal of Politics*, Vol. 24 (May, 1962), pp. 303–322.

[20] "The Changing Shape of the American Political Universe", *American Political Science Review*, Vol. 59 (March, 1965), p. 8.

[21] "Southern Images of Political Parties: An Analysis of White and Negro Attitudes", *Journal of Politics*, Vol. 26 (February, 1964), pp. 82–111. An expanded version of this article appears as "The Concept of Party Image and Its Importance for the Southern Electorate", in M. Kent Jennings and L. Harmon Zeigler, eds., *The Electoral Process* (Englewood Cliffs, N. J.: Prentice–Hall, 1965), pp. 139–174.

[22] "A Major Political Realignment in the South", in Allan P. Sindler, ed., *Change in the Contemporary South* (Durham, N. C.: Duke University Press, 1963), p. 195.

INTRODUCTION:

[1] See, for example, Austin Ranney and Willmore Kendall, *Democracy and the American Party System* (New York: Harcourt, Brace, 1956), pp. 155–166; Joseph A. Schlesinger, "A Two–Dimensional Scheme for Classifying the States According to Degree of Inter–Party Competition", *American Political Science Review*, Vol. 49 (September, 1955), pp. 1120–1128; and Edward F. Cox, "The Measurement of Party Strength", *Western Political Quarterly*, Vol. 13 (December, 1960), pp. 1022–1042.

[2] See Charles O. Jones, "The 1964 Presidential Election—Further Adventures in Wonderland", in

The American Government Annual 1965–66, ed. Donald G. Herzberg (New York: Holt, Rinehart, and Winston, 1965), pp. 8–10.

[3] Robert D. Novak, *The Agony of the G.O.P. in 1964* (New York: Macmillan Co., 1965), pp. 136–137. For elaborations of the southern strategy by Goldwater enthusiasts see, for example, Ralph de Toledano, *The Winning Side: The Case for Goldwater Republicanism* (New York: Macfadden Books, 1964); Dr. Thomas H. Brigham, formerly vice-chairman for urban areas, and Manyon M. Millican, formerly executive director of the Republican Party of Alabama, *Let's Face Facts: An Analysis for Future Republican Growth, 1964* (Mimeographed). For an interesting post–mortem analysis, also written by a Goldwater enthusiast, see Stephen Shadegg, *What Happened to Goldwater?* (New York: Holt, Rinehart, and Winston, 1965).

[4] Unless indicated otherwise, election returns used in this study are complete and official as reported by the secretaries–of–state of the eleven southern states.

[5] What is needed, of course, is an integrative approach in which the analytical strengths of both aggregative and survey data are fully exploited. In this regard, Walter Dean Burnham notes that the Survey Research Center is now developing a national electoral–data archive which, when completed, "should provide the material basis for a massive breakthrough in the behavioral analysis of American political history over the last century and a half". See "The Changing Shape of the American Political

Universe", *American Political Science Review*, Vol. 59 (March, 1965), p. 8.

[6] For a discussion of the relative research utility of survey data and aggregate data, see Angus Campbell, "Recent Developments in Survey Studies of Political Behavior", in *Essays on the Behavioral Studies of Politics*, ed. Austin Ranney (Urbana, Ill.: University of Illinois Press, 1962). Also see Campbell's "Voters and Elections: Past and Present", *The Journal of Politics*, Vol. 26 (November, 1964), pp. 745–757.

[7] James MacGregor Burns, *The Deadlock of Democracy* (Englewood Cliffs, N.J.: Prentice–Hall, 1963), p. 73.

CHAPTER I

[1] For analyses of black–belt voting in the elections of 1956 and 1960, see Donald S. Strong, *Urban Republicanism in the South* (University, Ala.: Bureau of Public Administration, 1960); and Bernard Cosman, "Presidential Republicanism in the South, 1960", *The Journal of Politics*, Vol. 24 (May, 1962), pp. 303–322.

CHAPTER II

[1] Negro registration data were provided by the U. S. Civil Rights Commission. See Table 6.

[2] The figures on religious affiliation used in this book are taken from the studies of *Churches and*

Church Membership in the United States, National Council of Churches of Christ in the U.S.A., 1957. Note that the Roman Catholic practice of including children in the computation of total membership inflates the Catholic proportion of a county's total population.

[3] For an analysis of the role of religion in Louisiana in 1960, see Bernard Cosman, "Religion and Race in Louisiana Presidential Politics, 1960", *The Southwestern Social Science Quarterly*, Vol. 43 (December, 1962), pp. 235–241.

[4] An analysis of Louisiana's "General Election, November, 1964", appears in *PAR Analysis* (Public Affairs Research Council of Louisiana), No. 123 (December, 1964).

[5] Negro registration might easily become a highly significant explanatory variable if it were possible to identify and remove from the data counties which had experienced heavy increases in Negro registration from 1948 to 1964.

[6] This study owes much to the generosity of the National Broadcasting Company and Mr. Harrison Lilly, director of NBC's Regional Election Center, Atlanta, Georgia, in making available these "Tag" data, as well as the "Tag" data from elsewhere in the South.

[7] *New York Times*, October 12, 1964.

[8] See V. O. Key, Jr. and Frank Munger, "Social Determinism and Electoral Decision: The Case of Indiana", in Eugene Burdick and Arthur Brodbeck, eds., *American Voting Behavior* (Glencoe, Ill.: The Free Press, 1959), pp. 281–299.

[9] *Politics, Parties, and Pressure Groups*, 5th ed. (New York: Crowell, 1964), p. 247.

[10] Charles Farris, "Effects of Negro Voting Upon the Politics of a Southern City: An Intensive Study, 1946–1948" (unpublished doctoral dissertation, University of Chicago, 1953); Samuel Lubell, *Revolt of the Moderates* (New York: Harper, 1956), pp. 185–186; and Bernard Cosman, "Republicanism in the Metropolitan South" (unpublished doctoral dissertation, University of Alabama, 1960).

[11] See Donald S. Strong, *Urban Republicanism in the South* and Bernard Cosman, "Presidential Republicanism in the South, 1960", *The Journal of Politics*, Vol. 24 (May, 1962), pp. 303–322.

[12] See Angus Campbell, Philip E. Converse, Warren E. Miller, and Donald E. Stokes, *The American Voter* (New York: Wiley, 1960), p. 338.

[13] Philip Converse, "A Major Political Realignment in the South" in Allan P. Sindler, ed., *Change in the Contemporary South* (Durham, N. C.: Duke University Press, 1963).

[14] Birmingham and other cities in which voting behavior was examined were chosen for analysis because at least some of their precinct or ward boundaries have remained fairly stable in recent years, making it possible to compare voting behavior in 1964 with that of earlier elections. The method employed to identify the racial and economic characteristics of precincts or wards involves relating data about individual blocks (based on the 1960 U. S. census of housing) to maps of the precincts or wards. The

method is described in detail in "Republicanism in the Metropolitan South" (see note 10 above). For purposes of the present study the criteria used to differentiate precincts or wards by race and home value were as follows: white, 90 per cent or more white occupancy; home value, upper, $25,000 plus; upper–middle, $20,000–$24,999; middle, $15,000–$19,999; lower–middle, $10,000–$14,999; lower, under $10,-000. Note that rental values were also computed for each electoral subdivision, making it possible to identify and discard precincts or wards having ambivalent characteristics such as high home values and low rents.

[15] For example, a disproportionate share of the Deep South Republican delegates and alternates who attended the 1964 Republican National Convention were upper–middle and upper–status whites. Of the more than 70 per cent of these people who responded to a mail questionnaire, about three–fourths of them strongly agreed with the proposition that "the government in Washington should stay out of the question of [racially] integrating the public schools", and about four–fifths thought the question of voting rights of Negroes should be left entirely to state and local governments. See Bernard Cosman, *The Case of the Goldwater Delegates: Deep South Republican Leadership* (University, Ala.: Bureau of Public Administration, 1966).

[16] Of course, race is only one of many factors entering into the electoral decision that may muffle polarization of the vote along status lines. In addition to habitual party loyalties, attitudes toward "charis-

matic" candidates like Eisenhower and emotionally–
charged issues such as religion are among the more
important of the short–term forces that may cut
across class lines and cause voters in a particular election to divide in ways different from voter–divisions
characteristic of elections in which domestic social–
welfare issues are uppermost in the minds of most
voters. For a discussion of "Short–Term Fluctuations
in Status Polarization", see *The American Voter*,
pp. 346–350.

[17] This measure is a varient of the method used on
survey data by Robert Alford, *Party and Society*
(New York: Rand McNally, 1963). It was modified
to fit aggregate data by M. Kent Jennings and Harmon
Zeigler, as reported in "Class, Party, and Race in
Four Types of Elections: The Case of Atlanta", a pa-
per presented at the Annual Meeting of the Southern
Political Science Association, November 12–14, 1964,
Durham, N. C. Jennings and Ziegler computed the
percentage–point difference between the vote at each
of six social class intervals, including a lower–class
Negro interval.

[18] While race pushed Goldwater ahead of Nixon,
one may go back four years and inquire whether the
same issue was not also one of the factors that kept
Nixon so close to Eisenhower. In their analysis of the
1964 election, Philip Converse and his associates
pointed out that a "small" subset of the Survey Research Center's sample "tended to associate Kennedy
somewhat with a pro–civil rights position, and Nixon
with more of a 'go–slow' approach . . .", *American*

Political Science Review, Vol. 59 (June, 1965), p. 329. It would be interesting to know exactly what proportion of the "small" subset hailed from the South.

CHAPTER III

[1] For early analyses of the 1964 presidential election in Virginia and Florida, see Ralph Eisenburg, "The 1964 Presidential Election in Virginia: A Political Omen?", The University of Virginia *News Letter* (April 15, 1965); and Elston Roady, "The 1964 Election in Florida: Some Early Observations", The Florida State University *Governmental Research Bulletin* (November, 1964). A later analysis is O. Douglas Weeks, *Texas in 1964—A One–Party State Again?* (Austin, Texas: Institute of Public Affairs, 1965).

[2] *The American Political Science Review*, Vol. 59 (June, 1965), pp. 321–336.

[3] Thus, in the city of Atlanta, Jennings and Zeigler found that Negro concentration related inversely to the Democratic presidential vote in 1960, even with party and class controlled. [See "Class, Party, and Race in Four Types of Elections . . .", note 17, Chapter 2, above.] In a non–Deep South city, Tallahassee, Florida, Russell Middleton found Negro voters dividing about evenly for Kennedy and Nixon. [See "The Civil Rights Issue for Presidential Voting Among Southern Negroes and Whites", *Socal Forces,* Vol. 40 (March, 1962), p. 211.] On the other hand, in their regionwide study of political attitudes, Donald

Matthews and James Prothro found the Negro vote
to be heavily Democratic, as Kennedy carried about
four–fifths of the Negro Democrats' vote, about three–
fourths of the Negro Independents' vote, and more
than a third of the Negro Republicans' vote. [See
Journal of Politics, Vol. 26 (February, 1964), pp.
82–111.]

[4] "What Happened in the South?", Southern Regional Council, November 15, 1964.

[5] V. O. Key, Jr., *Southern Politics* (New York:
Knopf, 1949), pp. 282–283.

[6] *Ibid.*, p. 283.

CHAPTER IV

[1] V. O. Key, Jr., *Public Opinion and American Democracy* (New York: Knopf, 1961), p. 104.

[2] Philip Converse, "A Major Political Realignment
in the South?", in Allan P. Sindler, ed., *Change in
the Contemporary South* (Durham, N. C.: Duke University Press, 1963), p. 196.

[3] A word about the computation of a "trend" line
may be helpful to readers not familiar with this statistical device. In this case the line was estimated by
the method of least squares. As V. O. Key, Jr., ex-
plains it, ". . . a line is drawn that best 'fits' the series
[of figures for the elections from 1920 to 1964] in
that the sum of the squares of the deviations of the
actual points of the series from the line so located is
at a minimum. The actual values of the series would

not cluster so closely about any *other* line. [Emphasis added.] A line so fitted is known as a line of regression." See V. O. Key, Jr., *A Primer of Statistics for Political Scientists* (New York: Knopf, 1964), pp. 35, 78–81, 85–88.

[4] Philip E. Converse, Aage R. Clausen, and Warren E. Miller, "Electoral Myth and Reality: The 1964 Election", *The American Political Science Review,* Vol. 57 (June, 1965), p. 330.

[5] Donald S. Strong raises the more basic question of the validity of party identification within the southern electoral context in his "Durable Republicanism in the South", in Sindler (ed.) *Change in the Contemporary South,* especially pp. 192–194. For the comments of Philip Converse see "A Major Political Realignment in the South", also appearing in this volume.

[6] "A Major Political Realignment in the South", p. 220.

[7] For a careful analysis of the Hill–Martin race in Alabama as a critical election, see Walter Dean Burnham, "The Alabama Senatorial Election of 1962: Return of Inter–Party Competition", *Journal of Politics,* Vol. 26 (November, 1964), pp. 798–892.

[8] "Some Dynamic Elements of Contests for the Presidency: The Goldwater Disaster in Context", a paper presented at the annual meeting of the American Political Science Association, September 7–11, 1965, in Washington, D. C.

[9] The writer seeks to examine some of the possible opportunities and probable dilemmas of Deep South Republican leadership in *The Case of the Goldwater*

Delegates (University, Ala.: Bureau of Public Administration, 1966).

[10] While substantial, these increases in turnout were well below those which occurred from 1948 to 1952 when the Deep South electorate expanded by 70.5 per cent and the non–Deep South electorate by 66.1 per cent.

[11] For discussions of the place of the peripheral voter in the national electorate, see Angus Campbell, "Surge and Decline: A Study of Electoral Change", *Public Opinion Quarterly* Vol. 24 (1960), pp. 397–418; and Walter Dean Burnham, "The Changing Shape of the American Political Universe", *American Political Science Review,* Vol. 59 (March, 1965), pp. 7–28.